D1488872

MINNESOTA DRAMA EDITIONS NO. 4
Edited by Tyrone Guthrie

THREE PLAYS BY ARMAND SALACROU

The World Is Round
When the Music Stops
Marguerite

ENGLISH VERSIONS BY
NORMAN STOKLE

Minneapolis
UNIVERSITY OF MINNESOTA PRESS IN ASSOCIATION
WITH THE MINNESOTA THEATRE COMPANY

PUBLISHED IN GREAT BRITAIN, INDIA, AND PAKISTAN
BY THE OXFORD UNIVERSITY PRESS, LONDON, BOM-
BAY, AND KARACHI, AND IN CANADA BY THE COPP
CLARK PUBLISHING CO. LIMITED, TORONTO

I thank Professor Kurt Weinberg for introducing me to the work of Salacrou.

I thank my wife, Susan, for her constant help in improving the manuscript.

N. S.

Introduction

To AN AMERICAN director or actor approaching this volume with an eye to presenting the plays, Salacrou may be hard to get hold of at first reading. The forms themselves seem familiar enough, but the large historical epic, the brittle sex comedy, and the moralizing domestic drama seem to come from different writers with totally different techniques and intents. Careful rereading, however, reveals obsessions common to all three (helpfully described in the translator's introductory essay) and, more important for the potential interpreters, an approach to character opposed to the normal approach of English-speaking dramatists.

Salacrou belongs with and in some ways anticipates the philosophic writers of existentialist drama. His Savonarola in *The World Is Round* and Camus' Caligula have more in common with each other than either character has with the real man whose name he bears. In preparing *The World Is Round* or *Caligula* it would be useless and probably dangerous for us to steep ourselves in a study of the actual Florentine fanatic or the actual Roman emperor. We would be tempted to inject values from real life into a selectively abstract intellectual construction, to enrich it subtextually with whatever picturesque psychological details we may have found in our sources. There could be no worse mistake.

The distinctive quality shared by the three plays is a lack, or rather a deliberate elimination, of what actors refer to as subtext. Since most American directors and performers thrive on subtext to the extent of minimizing the words of the text itself, it would be easy for us to get off on the wrong foot with Salacrou. We take it for granted that a character does not state his real feelings or understand his real motivations. All our energies go into supplying emotions of our own to fill out, modify, and often contradict the text. Our dramatists write with this activity in mind; their dialogue allows for the enrichments and distortions which will almost certainly be visited on it in the course of rehearsal. Not so Salacrou. The only motive which will tell his story and make his point is the motive baldly stated in the text. Changes of feeling come on the word which defines them. There is little opportunity to personalize, to substitute the performer's feelings for those of the character. To an American actor, these intellectually conceived figures may appear not to be living characters at all.

Salacrou would be the first to confirm this suspicion. He has proclaimed repeatedly that his characters are subjectively imagined, not objectively observed. To put it less metaphysically, they are conceived as steps in an argument or illustrations of a thesis, rather than portraits, and the actor's job is to win the argument rather than to bring the portrait to life. This does not mean that he must *not* bring it to life, but merely that he must make it live strictly within the terms required by the philosophic plan.

Only if we discipline ourselves, deny ourselves the opportunities for spectacular stage effects and startling neurotic acting, will the curious structure of *The World Is Round* work onstage.

Savonarola, who controls the fate of all the many characters in all their diverse actions, is never shown doing anything at all. We see him carrying on one-sided arguments with God and finally with his scarcely less communicative executioner. The rest of the large cast function as demonstrations of the points in this argument, leading to the conclusion that life is comically loathsome when God does not answer or reveal Himself. Even the lovers exist only to demonstrate the inadequacy of love as an absolute in a world that is no longer the center of the universe. Once the point is made, Silvio is slaughtered offstage in a parenthetical reference and Lucciana is not given even that summary attention. The people of Florence, whose sufferings and conspiracies have taken up the bulk of the evening, are dismissed in Savonarola's last misanthropic outburst as comic villains whose fate does not deserve to be shown to us. Throughout the play, the author avoids the scenes and confrontations we expect. He is unwilling to let us get involved with his characters except in their function as points in Savonarola's desperate debate with the silence of God.

In staging *The World Is Round* (or *Caligula* or *The Flies* or *God and the Devil*) we are tempted to exploit spectacle for its own sake and to compensate for what we fear is too cerebral a script by fleshing it out with diffuse emotion. This temptation has corrupted a number of English and American productions of French philosophic plays. The time is coming, one hopes, when we shall be willing to subordinate our impulsive creativity to the precise demands of these tightly reasoned texts.

At first glance *When the Music Stops* seems to offer an opportunity for improvisational freedom, but even in this very funny sex farce Salacrou demands a rigorous adherence to the through line. A skillful and seemingly frivolous comedy of adultery, it ends shockingly in frustration, renunciation, and suicide. Two wives leave their husbands for lovers. One wife is sent home by her disgusted lover; the other returns voluntarily to her husband, and her deserted lover shoots himself. Nothing could be more natural than to motivate this series of sexual failures in private, clinical terms, with infinite gradations of passion and frigidity, ardor and impotence, but here again the point is likely to get lost in subjective elaboration. Salacrou is saying that the spectacle of somebody else's sins or compromises makes us hate our own and arouses in us the dormant guilt feelings and nostalgia for purity that we thought we had got rid of when we got rid of God. This motive must be the principal and in many cases the only cause for the seemingly arbitrary changes of heart if the play is to take the leap from frivolity to high seriousness which the author has daringly imagined.

Marguerite offers fewer temptations to go wrong than the other two. The thesis is presented in the terms of realistic emotional melodrama, and it can hardly be missed by any actor attuned to work on daytime television. Even here, however, the story is as improbable as the parables of Pirandello, but as in Pirandello, the impossible can carry conviction when acted naturalistically in the familiar style of domestic drama. There is no danger of conflict between the actor's full-throated passion and what has to be said.

These stageworthy translations of Salacrou should be of interest to American producers, now less parochial than ever before, and should help us to understand the special interpretive demands of a major modern dramatic tradition subtly but radically different from our own.

INTRODUCTION by Stephen Porter
page vii

ARMAND SALACROU AND HIS THEATRE
page 3

Selected Bibliography page 23

PLAYS

The World Is Round *page 27*

When the Music Stops *page 109*

Marguerite *page 191*

THREE PLAYS BY
ARMAND SALACROU

NORMAN STOKLE

Armand Salacrou and His Theatre

Aʀᴍᴀɴᴅ Sᴀʟᴀᴄʀᴏᴜ is widely recognized as one of the most significant dramatists in the twentieth-century French theatre. During the past four decades, his plays have attracted considerable attention in many parts of the world and been translated into a dozen languages. Yet for some unaccountable reason, they remain virtually unknown to English-speaking audiences. This, the first volume of his work to be published in English, constitutes an attempt to rectify, in some measure, that deficiency.

Salacrou was born at Rouen in 1899 but spent most of his childhood in Le Havre where his father was a druggist and active in local politics. Strongly influenced by his father's friends, by the local longshoremen and factory workers, Salacrou rejected religious faith at an early age, read radical political tracts, and, in 1916, founded an organization of "Young Socialists" in Le Havre. That same year, his first literary effort, a short story, "L'Eternelle chanson des gueux," was published in *L'Humanité.* After briefly studying medicine, he read philosophy at the Sorbonne, taking his *licence* in 1920 and his *diplôme d'études supérieures* in the following year with a thesis on Benedetto Croce. He married, and while eking out a living first as a journalist, then as an assistant film director, joined a group of Surrealist poets and painters. Masson, Gris, Miro, Tzara, and Artaud were among its leading members, and it was they who encouraged Salacrou to write for the theatre. His early dramatic efforts, strongly influenced by Surrealism, were all failures, but attracted the attention of Charles Dullin who was striving to regenerate the French theatre at his recently founded experimental Atelier. Disenchanted with his work in films, Salacrou accepted Dullin's offer of an administrative post, and a long and fruitful friendship developed between the two men. *Atlas-Hôtel*, presented by Dullin in 1931, brought Salacrou his first success. And this was followed by a series of plays — *Une Femme libre* (1934), *L'Inconnue d'Arras* (1935), *Un Homme comme les autres* (1936), *La Terre est ronde* (1938), and *Histoire de rire* (1939) — which established his reputation as a leading French dramatist.

Before these successes, Salacrou had founded a publicity agency in order to supplement his salary at the Atelier. This business enterprise proved extremely successful, and within a few years, he controlled a budget equal to that of Citroën. Having achieved financial independence, he sold the agency in 1938 to devote his time exclusively to writing.

At the outbreak of World War II, he enlisted in the army as a private, was taken prisoner near Brest in 1940, but soon escaped to Vichy France. During his long sojourn in Lyon, he wrote *La Marguerite* and *Les Fiancés du Havre*, and worked for the clandestine press. Following the Liberation, as director of the Théâtre de l'Odéon, he staged several of his own works in cooperation with Jean-Louis Barrault. Then, in 1949, Salacrou was elected to the Académie Goncourt, and in the same year

4

met Yves Robert who, with Barrault, became one of his important associates after the death of Dullin. *Les Nuits de la colère* (1946), *L'Archipel Lenoir* (1947), *Une Femme trop honnête* (1953), and *Boulevard Durand* (1960) are among Salacrou's more significant works of the postwar period. His recent writings include *Comme les chardons* (1964), *La Dernière rencontre* (1965), and two volumes of memoirs and meditations on life: *Les Idées de la nuit* (1960) and *Impromptu délibéré* (1966). Now residing in Le Havre, Salacrou is currently preparing a new volume of "Réflexions sur la vie."

The thirty plays which Salacrou has so far written constitute a record of his search for a meaning to life, a projection of his anxiety before the enigma of existence. Lacking faith, yet recognizing the need for God's existence if human life is to be something more than an intolerable hell of absurdity, Salacrou strives, through his theatre, to force God into an "imprudence divine," thereby revealing Himself as if by accident. No revelation is induced, and since for Salacrou there is no alternative, he leaves his characters floundering in the nihilistic abyss between Christianity and Sartrian humanism.

The same themes are in evidence during every stage in the development of Salacrou's work: the need for God's revelation; the moral problems arising from God's absence; the rejection of reality; the inadequacy of language in human relations; solitude; death. However, two distinct phases are discernible in his evolution as a dramatist. The first phase, extending from 1923 to 1938, is dominated by his desperate attempts to promote a divine revelation. It can be further divided into two parts on the basis of dramatic technique, his plays before 1930 being strongly influenced by Surrealism, those after 1930 moving closer to Naturalism in both dramatic situation and characterization. Salacrou's greatest success as a dramatist came during this 1930–38 period, ironically, at the time of his deepest business involvement. The second phase, from 1939 to the present, is more particularly preoccupied with the moral and social problems to which the absence of God gives rise. It is marked by an ever-deepening nihilism as Salacrou quietly reconciles himself to the fact of life's futility and embraces the theory of determinism in nature. While sharing the nausea of Sartre in face of the "absurd," Salacrou, unlike him, rejects the notion that man can exercise free will: "I certainly do not deny that our decisions are motivated, but I see no more in these motives than causes and effects. My motives do not rise up brand-new, original, out of nothing. They themselves are motivated, born of parents as we are. They come linked one with the other; circumstances and chance deform them — and what we call chance is the intervention of forces outside of ourselves. And I, myself, become the 'chance' of others, and in the chain, a cause of their decisions and their history." (*Théâtre*, VI (1954), p. 211.) The acceptance of such a determinist view places Salacrou in a moral dilemma. If man is governed by forces beyond his control, he can hardly be held responsible for his acts. Where, then, must the responsibility be placed? Salacrou has not been able to resolve this question satisfactorily. Rejecting the clearly defined absolutes of religious and political ideologies or the more tentative man-based "philosophy of limits" advocated by Camus, Salacrou lacks a basis upon which to make moral judgments. The world of his plays is one of multiple truths. "What others call my lies are my truths of the previous day or of my other existences," declares Ade in *Histoire de rire*. Since to judge presupposes the existence of an absolute and freedom of choice on the part of the judged one, Salacrou urges that judgment be replaced by understanding and compassion. "We must have pity for men and women today," says Madame Berthe in *Un Homme comme les autres*, "for they hurt one another and cannot be held guilty." Helplessly searching for a happiness they can never know, nostalgic for the youthful innocence they no longer possess, Salacrou's characters are spectators of their own predetermined lives, waiting with great curiosity to discover what their destiny will be.

Salacrou is, nevertheless, acutely aware of the dangers inherent in the refusal to pronounce moral judgments. And, despite their lack of faith, his characters often continue to employ Christian values in judging themselves and others. Their unending torment stems from this paradox, since they are "determined" robots endowed with a Christian conscience, devoid of the free will to choose their acts, yet compelled to judge them according to the Christian ethic as if such free will existed.

Purity, especially viewed in sexual terms, is as dominant a theme in Salacrou's work as it is in Anouilh's. He litters his plays with adulterous and sordid women whose choice of mate for their sexual gratification is frequently a matter of complete indifference. Every woman in every play in this volume, for instance, practices illicit coition usually without any concomitant feeling of guilt. Whereas the women in Salacrou's decidedly misogynic theatre are earthy sexual objects with their hands deep in the mud of elemental living, the men are romantic dreamers who crave an unattainable purity. Compatibility between the sexes is impossible, for one of the partners is constantly shattering the hopes and dreams of the other. Louis and Gerald, in *Histoire de rire*, reject Helen and Nicole respectively; Silvio, in *La Terre est ronde*, rejects Lucciana, while Savonarola rejects all women, including his own mother. The converse is true in *La Marguerite*. It is Marguerite who becomes the romantic, searching for purity, and finally rejecting her adulterous doctor for the unsullied memory of her dead husband. Consumed by self-interest, acting exclusively in accord with their private welfare and glory, Salacrou's characters live in a multiplicity of separate worlds, each governed by its own laws and propelled by forces that other human beings either cannot understand or have no desire to understand. As private illusions are confused with reality, and meaningful contacts rendered impossible, the sexual act becomes a substitute for real communication.

More the product of his metaphysical anguish and moral preoccupations than of his observations, Salacrou's characters exist as attitudes rather than as living beings with whom the audience can identify. In his "Lettre aux critiques" (*Revue de l'Œuvre*, Winter 1926), he commented: "I do not seek to observe life but to give it; my characters, you live in me, not in the street . . . you are merely the notes of my soul." However, since Salacrou's problems are common to many other human beings, the "notes of his soul" have perhaps a more general validity. He believes, as did Rimbaud, that "Je est un autre," and that through the revelation of his authentic being he may help his fellows to see the reality of their condition and discover new truths.

Ionesco's view of the theatre expressed in *L'Impromptu de l'Alma* closely approximates that of Salacrou: "For me, the theatre is the projection on-stage of the inner world: it is in my dreams, my anguish, my obscure desires, and my interior contradictions that I, for my part, reserve the right to find my dramatic material. As I am not alone in the world, as each one of us in the depths of his being is at the same time everyone else, my dreams, my desires, my anguish, and my obsessions do not belong to me personally; they form part of an ancestral heritage, a very old store which constitutes the domain of all humanity." (*Théâtre*, II (Paris: Gallimard, 1958), p. 57.)

Strongly influenced by Surrealism, Salacrou (especially in his earlier plays) and Ionesco have contested the Aristotelian rules of logical causality in action and character portrayal. Both have constructed circular plots, freed from chronological time, in order to voice their antipathy for "bourgeois" smugness and to

8

present their poetic image of the human predicament. But whereas in the plays of the agnostic Ionesco the awareness of life's futility can often lead to a counter-feeling of great joy before the beauties of the world, no such reaction penetrates the ubiquitous pessimism of a play by Salacrou. The latter, always a candidate for religious faith, approaches the theatre as a ritual during which he may perhaps feel the possibility of salvation. "For myself, it is at the theatre, in certain moments of great purity, that I have felt closest to reaching the inaccessible shore. And it is in the greatest works of drama that I have sometimes thought I have found my salvation." (*Théâtre*, II (1944), p. 228.) For Salacrou, as for his former friend Artaud, "The theatre is the Land of Fire, lagoon of Sky, battle of Dreams. Theatre is Solemn Ceremony . . . the unlimited domain of the spirit." (From a letter by Artaud to the director of the Comédie-Française written in 1925. A translation of the letter appears in the *Tulane Drama Review*, VIII, No. 2 (Winter 1963), p. 43.) But it is also, in Salacrou's case, the domain of metaphysical and moral chaos where nothing ultimately has meaning except solitude and death.

The three plays in this volume are representative of Salacrou's maturest work. *The World Is Round* (*La Terre est ronde*), considered by many critics as the author's finest achievement, is now in the permanent repertory of the Comédie-Française. It was during a trip to Italy, in 1920, that Salacrou first became interested in Savonarola and sketched a five-act play dramatizing the history of his theocracy in Florence (1492–98). The final version, however, was only completed in 1937. Replete with all the ingredients necessary for a gripping drama, the subject was also particularly suited to projecting Salacrou's own metaphysical anguish, his social and moral concerns. Human isolation, hypocrisy, death, the conflicts between faith and reason, the spiritual and the sensual, immorality and arbitrary morality

— such themes had always been prominent in his theatre. But now, in Savonarola's Florence, Salacrou discovered the ground on which all of these themes could be synthesized with complete authenticity. It was undoubtedly the ending of the story which attracted Salacrou most, for Savonarola's final doubt and despair reflected his own, and gave support to his ever-deepening belief in the utter futility of human existence.

The historical facts, from Savonarola's sudden rise to power with his pacification of the French invaders to his rejection of the red hat and final martyrdom, formed an almost perfect dramatic trajectory. History had also furnished a whole array of secondary figures almost as fascinating as Savonarola himself to assist in unfolding the drama. Fra Francesco da Puglia, a Franciscan friar who had challenged him to an ordeal by fire, emerged as the comical Fra Mariano; Fra Domenico, nicknamed Brother Factotum, Savonarola's most devoted disciple who, confusing moral and physical courage, accepted the challenge in his master's stead, was transformed into Silvio. The latter, a romantic idealist, would duplicate — though for more complex reasons — Fra Domenico's silent torture and death. There was the children's militia with its Nazi tactics, and the barbarian French invaders, at once menacing and comical. By creating Minutello's family and friends, representing all strata of society from the wealthy merchant and professional classes to artisans, domestics, and young dilettantes, Salacrou provided a composite of the various Florentine attitudes to the theocracy. His main problem was one of dramatic structure: how to reduce six extremely eventful years into the space of one evening, and show the growing conflict between Florence and Rome while avoiding unnecessary character proliferation and disjointedness in plot development. One may well take issue with Salacrou for his method of condensing history. The material he has eliminated is certainly as dramatic as the material he has included. Savonarola's dealings with the French king, his refusal to administer the last rites to Lorenzo of Medici, the great climax of the ordeal by fire, all have been set aside and merely reported at second hand. More than that, Savonarola himself remains outside of the central drama as a sort of unintegrated chorus-figure. What, then, was Salacrou's intention? As the title of his play indicates, it was not primarily to dramatize the story of Florence's thaumaturgical monk, but to demonstrate his own nihilistic view of the human condition. Seen in this light, Salacrou's selection of historical details becomes more understandable. Minutello's household may be interpreted as a symbol for all mankind whose drama is essentially ours.

The problem of how to portray the conflict between Florence and Rome was resolved by the creation of Faustina. Being at once Minutello's wayward daughter and an intimate of Pope Alexander, she is the all-important pivotal figure linking the two opposing camps of San Marco and the Vatican. As her name suggests, she is the "evil" one, the corrupt extension of Rome. Her function is threefold: to render Silvio unacceptable as a son-in-law to Minutello; to bring Savonarola's Florence into clearer perspective by contrasting it with her adopted city; and, as the Pope's agent, to precipitate the denouement. Through Faustina, we see the papal court, worldly, amoral, indulgent, sophisticated in its tastes, appreciative of art and luxury — in short, the exact antipode of theocratic Florence where the sexes are separated, works of art consigned to the bonfire, and all but the simple necessities of life denied to the populace. Since historically the Vatican had repeatedly reminded the Florentine citizenry that Savonarola's prophetic claims were unsupported by miraculous powers, Salacrou, having firmly integrated Faustina into Act I, could safely allow her to instigate the clamor for a miracle while avoiding a *deus ex machina*.

Savonarola emerges as a schizophrenic. His fiery yet strangely

11

disjointed eloquence pushes him beyond reason and sanity in search of the miraculous. He is a man of many parts — prophet, reformer, child, misanthropist, man of God, God himself — and his long soliloquies constitute a series of transformations from one part to the next, or at times even a dialogue between two different parts. Such a characterization cannot be altogether dismissed as an attempt by Salacrou, the unbeliever, to discredit Savonarola, a man of seemingly boundless faith; for these soliloquies are, to a considerable extent, reproductions of the friar's own words as recorded by history.

Despising the corruption and decadence of the Church in general and of Florentine society in particular, Savonarola wishes to purify his people and lead them back into the fold of the truly faithful. To convince himself and others that he is an instrument of God's will, he seeks an intimate, personal relationship with the Creator. As he talks to God and hears His replies, one begins to suspect the good monk's motives. Is his desire to give Florence to God as a pure flower perhaps no more than a lust for earthly power? Savonarola is at least subliminally aware that if he can enjoy a special relationship with God from which the rest of the population is excluded, he will be the most exalted of men and have the means to dominate his city's affairs. He exerts every effort to achieve this relationship, or rather, to convince the city, and more especially himself, of its achievement.

When he hears the voice of God, he hears, in fact, only the sound of his own voice as he fashions the Creator into his alter ego. For Savonarola, as for Faustina, God is a parrot who can do no more than echo the words man has taught Him to speak. The will of God now completely identified with that of Savonarola, the latter is ready to do battle with those terrestrial opponents who bar his way to absolute power. This undertaking is decidedly more complex since Lorenzo of Medici, the Pope, and the population of Florence have wills of a more tangible nature and cannot be so easily subjugated. Yet circumstances play into Savonarola's hands. Lorenzo is on his deathbed, and his heir, Piero, has little interest in politics. The monk prophesies death for the already succumbing Prince of Florence, refuses him the last rites of the Church, then saves the city from devastation by the invading French army. Convinced of Savonarola's divine inspiration, the local population at last acknowledges the value that he has long claimed for himself, thereby clearing the way for the establishment of his totalitarian regime.

Although Savonarola's power depends upon the support of the masses, for him to admit this limitation would be tantamount to settling for something less than absolutism. Hence, he cultivates the image of self-sufficiency and infallibility, acting as if the power of the people does not exist. He becomes a God-figure, and his power in Florence, now based on a double illusion, is secure. But Florence is not Italy, and Savonarola still owes allegiance to the Pope. Despite his excellent prospects of one day assuming the papal crown, his thirst for immediate, absolute power is unquenchable. At this critical juncture, fortune again smiles on Savonarola as the Pope, in a conciliatory gesture, offers him a cardinalship. To accept the red hat, however, would be to destroy the illusion Savonarola has created for himself, since it would imply recognition of Borgia's superiority. By rejecting the ecclesiastical princedom, he proves to himself and to Florence that he is indeed superior to Borgia.

No sooner is Savonarola's power consolidated than its base begins to crumble. After six years of unnatural living, even the passive Florentines need more than words as a sign of their ruler's special relationship with God. They need visible proof, and Savonarola's failure to grant them a miracle breaks the double illusion and ends his regime. Deserted by his flock, tortured and disfigured in his cell, he vaguely perceives that God is just another name for himself. He has simply glorified and worshiped

13

his own reflection in the void of infinity. Filled with hatred for man in a world as purposeless as universal gravitation, Savonarola utters his last, nihilistic shout: "All is comedy and the comedy is over." His life and doctrine seemingly repudiated, he waits for death at the end of a rope.

Like a host of other post-romantic heroes, Silvio is searching for a purpose in life. Living in a decadent, corrupt society which, before the advent of Savonarola, has lost its spiritual and moral direction, he yearns for a way out of the "absurd" and for purity in his relationships with others. From the outset, he is clearly excellent material for Savonarola's convent. However, having failed to diagnose his problem sufficiently, Silvio has no clear idea how it should be resolved. While feeling dissatisfaction with the present order of things, he, like Anouilh's Becket, agrees to live in that order until a better alternative presents itself. In his efforts to give substance to his existence, he arranges to accompany Amerigo Vespucci on his voyage of discovery to the New World. There, perhaps, he will find new truths and a new direction. But ultimately, sensing that his geographical wanderings will not resolve his metaphysical or moral problems, he avoids the North American disillusion of a Des Grieux or a René.

His brave attempt to cultivate a "pure" love for Lucciana, untarnished by sexual indulgence, ends in failure when Lucciana herself, no longer able to withhold her favors, seduces him. His "pure" love sullied forever, the disillusioned Silvio deserts her for a life of untrammeled debauchery. One of his numerous "excesses" is to attend the church of San Marco. But instead of mocking Savonarola, he is enthralled by him. At the moment of his deepest despair, he stumbles upon the highest purity of all: the purity of the spirit. The road to San Marco is Silvio's greatest voyage of discovery. Savonarola's Dominican convent affords Silvio not only the prospect of personal salvation but also the possibility of being reunited in spiritual purity with his beloved Lucciana, now married to Manente. Deprived of his possession, Silvio sees in his faith the only way of reclaiming it. He tells his former mistress: "Our life together on earth was no longer possible, Lucciana, yet I couldn't bear to lose you. I had to believe in immortality so that you could be immortal."

While waiting for a happy reunion with Lucciana in the next life, Silvio uses the political power he enjoys as Savonarola's protégé to restore her to a state of purity. Repulsed by the haunting vision of her lovemaking with Manente, he does all in his power to destroy the marriage. He has Manente arrested and whipped; he urges Lucciana to enter a convent, and although she refuses, she nevertheless agrees to live "as a widow" in Manente's house. Since Silvio defines purity almost exclusively in sexual terms, he feels he has won a great victory. For, in removing Lucciana from Manente's bed, he has, in some measure, regained her for himself. Yet he is well aware that his triumph can only be sustained by Savonarola's continued domination over Florence. Since Lucciana's abstinence depends upon the political fortunes of his master, and since their future reunion requires his dedication to Savonarola's cause, Silvio will support him to the end.

Silvio's motives for embracing the faith are thus open to censure. Like his master, he gives himself to the Church largely for his own ulterior purposes, and like him, cultivates the illusion of faith even in face of torture and death. Savonarola is a martyr to the cause of personal power; Silvio is a martyr for Lucciana. Here is the supreme irony. Neither martyrdom is explainable in terms of God since both men have merely harnessed religion to the service of their own earthly gods. The condemned Savonarola is not blind to his disciple's motives in choosing death when he cries: "Now my work will perish because you had to save one solitary woman. Yours is not a saintly nature, Silvio. . . ."

Paradoxically, from the moment Silvio abandons Lucciana, it is she who unwittingly governs his every action, for she has become his absolute. Even as a monk, he can tell her: ". . . if my eternal damnation could give you entry to Paradise, Lucciana, I should damn myself that you might be saved and might still think of me when you were alone before God." These are the words of a hero rather than of a saint. Savonarola is right. Yet he does not condemn his disciple, because to a large degree, Silvio is a mirror of himself.

The question of moral values in a godless society constitutes a central theme of the play. It is precisely Minutello's moral inconsistency which triggers the main action of the drama. His attempts to preserve the moral uprightness of his two daughters while openly encouraging the masked woman to indulge in fornication prompt Silvio's bitter reaction which, in turn, renders impossible the latter's marriage to Lucciana. But such moral inconsistency is by no means the monopoly of Minutello. In the first scene of the play, Giaccomo, excited by the prospect of coitus with the woman he has just met, is reduced to tears when he realizes she is a common prostitute. Later, the French army, while respecting the dignity of its own people, is perfectly happy to rape, loot, and exterminate the local populations of Italy. And like Giaccomo, even the lowly Cognac longs to rape "decent" women. Self-interest is the only morality, the only motivating force. This factor, more than any other, explains the remarkable durability of Savonarola's regime. The people whom he rules are so inward-looking, so incapable of seeing beyond themselves, that they fail to present a combined opposition against him. His downfall results from the "external" — though far from disinterested — intervention of Faustina who, now able to objectify the Florentine situation, sees in her "proof by fire" a way to win further gifts from the Pope. In the lethal conflict between Savonarola's God-oriented medievalism and the progressive forces of the Italian Renaissance, it is the amoral Faustina who poses the essential enigma: "I can understand man's desire to create God in order to find comfort and an explanation for everything from the stars to his own emotions. But what I do not understand is that one day, in the great void, God had the desire to create man." The interminable silence of a God whose existence remains forever in doubt and the double martyrdom at the end of the play leave Florence sighing with relief and free to return to its decadent normality as the star of Machiavelli rises over the horizon.

When the Music Stops (*Histoire de rire*) and *Marguerite* (*La Marguerite*), which belong to the second major phase in Salacrou's development, are devoted to an investigation of the moral problems arising from God's absence. On what basis, asks Salacrou, can atheistic man continue to justify his adherence to a Christian morality? Rejection of the faith must surely invalidate the morality which is dependent upon it. But what is there to take its place?

By constructing the action of *When the Music Stops* around two couples, each seeing its own state mirrored in the other, Salacrou is able to demonstrate this problem of moral ambiguity with great poignancy. Louis, while having an affair with Helen, wife of Jules, tries desperately to prevent Gerald's wife, Ade, from doing the same thing with Achilles. Gerald's favorable attitude toward Helen's adultery does not apply in the case of his own wife. Only when he discovers Ade's infidelity does his moral attitude become consistent for all women. Then, he despises both Helen and Nicole because they mirror the sins of his own wife. And those sins haunt him. Like Silvio, Gerald is obsessed for many sleepless nights by the image of his loved one giving herself to another. Helen, though ever willing to deceive her husband, is very upset by Louis' suggestion that Jules might well have a mistress of his own.

17

The play develops into a courtroom trial with each character, in turn, passing moral judgment on another for the sins he himself has committed. In this respect, it resembles the hell of Sartre's *Huis-Clos*, save that the basis for judgment is Christian rather than existential. Having passed beyond romanticism, Jules judges no one. He alone is capable of holding life at a distance and analyzing its moral problems realistically. "Today, my friend, religion means nothing to our wives," he tells Gerald. "And whose fault is it? Do we go to church? No. And so the only morality left to them is 'love,' the most uncertain, most ill-defined word in the human vocabulary." His analysis amounts to a dispassionate restatement of Savonarola's final anguished enunciation: if God does not exist, then all is comedy. Jules is simply more resigned to life's comedy. The other male characters, however, are unable to share his detachment. Gerald, Louis, and Achilles find reality as painful as did Silvio, and like him, reject it to construct illusionary worlds of their own. Gerald and Achilles both fabricate their personal image of Ade; Louis' image of Helen is similarly divorced from reality. Following in the steps of Savonarola and Silvio, they believe only what they want to believe concerning the object of their affections and invest that object with absolute powers. Consequently, each lives in his separate, impenetrable compartment, spins his own dreams, and has no understanding of his mate.

When circumstances no longer permit the illusions to be sustained, catastrophe results. Ade leaves Achilles and he attempts suicide; Jules reveals Helen's true character and Louis bitterly rejects her; Gerald, the first to be disillusioned, senses the acute anguish involved in glimpsing reality, and deliberately chooses to resuscitate his original, less painful illusions. As he puts it: "When you've known real suffering, even false happiness seems sweet." At the end of the play, Gerald emerges relatively unscathed, having avoided coming to terms either with himself or

his situation. He is the most pathetic figure of all because he has learned nothing from his experience and has merely postponed his day of reckoning. The disillusioned Louis, with greater courage, pays the high price for sustaining the reality he has finally grasped — the price Gerald recognized and refused to pay — namely, the rejection of society for a solitary life in the wilderness. Louis' motives resemble those of Anouilh's Gaston rather than those of Molière's Alceste. Yet whereas Gaston suddenly finds himself with the means to live in permanent, luxurious seclusion, Louis cannot reasonably expect such enormous good fortune. He is young, talented, and with a promising future ahead of him. He will register his brief protest. Then Gerald will restore him to society as surely as Philinte will restore Alceste.

The essential conflict in this play, as in the later *Marguerite*, stems from the differing levels of moral consciousness in the main protagonists. This difference is clearly distinguishable on the basis of sex. No matter how derelict in their connubial duties, no matter how liberal in their extramarital relationships, the women seem remarkably immune from all feelings of guilt. All of the men, on the other hand, are deeply concerned with the morality of their respective situations. At once lovers and cuckolds, Gerald, Louis, and Achilles interact with one another and duplicate each other's experience. Gerald looks to Jules for comfort in the face of their common situation. Louis sees himself in the abandoned Achilles who has fired the gun in his stead. The source of their anguish is to be found in their common, unsatisfied need for a clear moral code by which to regulate their actions. It is the older, wiser Jules, having already lived their experience, who can tell them that their problem has no solution in a world without God. At the end of the play, the situation of the beginning is reversed as the inconstant wives return to their lawful mates leaving Achilles and Louis in the position they had originally intended for Gerald and Jules. But this vicious game of love without rules has no victors. Gerald, Achilles, and Louis are all at different stages along the same road of moral anarchy which ultimately leads to suicide or the quiet wisdom of Jules.

As the men mirror each other, so do the women. Young, rich, childless, utterly bored by the mundane gestures of everyday life and isolated because of their selfishness, Ade, Helen, and Nicole long for a life of excitement and passionate fulfillment instead of the deadening respectability to which their marriages have condemned them. Discarding their husbands like old toys, they seize upon "love" as a means of escape from their vacuous lives. And that escape is greatly facilitated by their underdeveloped moral conscience in regard to their own behavior. This deficiency is both their greatest source of power over their morally conscious partners, and the cause of their downfall. Invested with the power to control the happiness or misery of their menfolk, they can dominate the relationship and manipulate it on their own terms. Ultimately, this power renders the relationship uninteresting to them because it loses its challenge. Their lovers gradually resembling their abandoned husbands, the women withdraw to their ever-forgiving spouses while examining the field for their next adulterous match. The vicious circle is complete. Only when their domination is questioned, as when Ade sees her husband at the casino with Nicole, does the relationship recapture its challenge. Then, Ade, insufferably bored by her unchallenged empire over Achilles, hurries back to re-establish her domination over the seemingly too independent Gerald. The men, too monopolized by moral considerations to serve as worthy opponents in the inter-sexual war, see little to distinguish one woman from the other. All are amoral sluts, undeserving of their love and trust.

Ade, Helen, and Nicole live for the present moment with its immediate pleasures, unable or unwilling to stop the party for a confrontation with their own conscience. Perhaps they suspect that to achieve self-definition is to discover the void at the center of their lives. Until they lose their sexual attractiveness, they must continue to play their escapist games. After that, there will be time enough for moral causes and moments of truth. In the meantime, Ade and Helen will become more like Nicole, for their road is essentially hers. There will be more skiing trips for Helen, and more foreign travel. Ade, the great romantic with the blood of 1830 in her veins, has thoroughly enjoyed her first adventure. Having taught Gerald to accept her on her own terms, she will continue to create havoc, as did her grandmother, in order to avoid the drabness of everyday living, while Gerald, resembling more and more the philosophical Jules, sinks back in his chair to read *The Times*.

Whereas *When the Music Stops* belongs to the tradition of boulevard farce, *Marguerite*, while developing the same themes, is more serious in tone. In this latter play, it is the young widow, Marguerite, who now resembles Silvio and Gerald in her spurning of sordid reality for illusion.

Her blind father-in-law recalls, with a mixture of relish, pride, and disgust, his former debaucheries in the nearby ditches. He envies his son, Paul, who, far from his own village, can spurn respectability and moral restraint and give full play to his most basic drives. Yet he objurgates his own daughter-in-law when he suspects she might be enjoying the same sexual freedoms under his own roof. In the old patriarch, the club of moral inconsistency has found a new member.

The reality in which the old man finds himself is as intolerable to him as Silvio's or Gerald's reality was to them. To accept his son's death is to lose his last remaining purpose in life, to enter a world without hope. Consequently, he rejects the reality of his situation in order to construct one of his own which allows him to believe in Paul's imminent return. To sustain his illusion, he requires everyone else to share it and to act accordingly. He insists Marguerite lay out Paul's black suit for him; he tries to thwart Marguerite's "adultery" with the doctor; he talks incessantly of Paul's return. But Marguerite and her doctor-friend remain unconvinced, choosing to face present realities instead of phantoms from the past. Both can find happiness together as man and wife. Their dedication is to the living, not the dead.

The arrival of the visitor, whom the blind old man mistakes for Paul, fills Marguerite with hope and fear; hope, because with his son's return, the old man will be able to die promptly and in peace, leaving her free to marry the doctor; fear, lest the old man discover the error which she is helping to foster and become an even more cantankerous tyrant. The chances of discovery seem great, since the visitor is an utter stranger to the family, knows nothing of their circumstances, and has little to gain from being Marguerite's accomplice. The dramatic interest of the play thus centers around the question of whether or not the old man's illusion can be sustained. But the uncertainty is more apparent than real, for the old man has already decided to believe the visitor is Paul, and Marguerite's complicity is scarcely necessary. He can take his illusion to the grave. That, indeed, is all he seeks.

Yet ironically, the old patriarch's death, far from bringing an end to his regime, simply reaffirms it. Marguerite has realized that the doctor means nothing to her and that her love for Paul is still very much alive. Knowing that if her husband ever returned, she would beg his forgiveness for her illicit relations with the doctor, she embraces the old man's illusion, and like him, waits alone for someone who will never come. As she falls to her knees, calling softly for her drowned husband, Marguerite becomes, like Silvio, a sacrifice to the purity of her love.

The three plays in this volume summarize the major concerns of Salacrou's theatre as a whole. All his plays, whether constructed in the form of farce, comedy, or serious drama, have deeply tragic implications since they all have the same purpose: to diagnose the tragedy of life itself. Salacrou does not presume to offer any solutions. It is rather for each individual to find his own. "All my work, in its better moments," he affirms, "is simply a shout to awaken those who are asleep, to disturb them; a metaphysical or social protest against the contentment of living. . . ." (*Théâtre*, VI, pp. 98–99.) Serious as his purpose may be, he shares with Molière, Anouilh, and Ionesco the gift for making his audiences laugh heartily as they receive his bitter rational judgments. But while there is bitterness in his theatre, there is also warmth, tenderness, and sympathy for his suffering fellow man. If we must forgive God for the life He has chosen us to lead, says Salacrou, then surely we must afford our fellow human beings the greatest tolerance.

Selected Bibliography

Works of Armand Salacrou

Théâtre. 8 volumes. Paris: Gallimard, 1943–66.
La Boule de verre, in *Intentions* (Paris), Nos. 28–30 (December 1924).
Magasin d'accessoires, in *Sélection* (Antwerp), No. 10 (July 1925).
"A Message to the American Educational Theatre," *Educational Theatre Journal*, III, No. 1 (March 1951).
A Pied, au-dessus des nuages. Paris: Seghers, 1956.
Les Idées de la nuit. Paris: Fayard, 1960.
Pièces à lire: Les Trente Tombes de Judas, Histoire de Cirque, in *Les Œuvres Libres*, No. 173 (October 1960).
A Circus Story (play for reading), in *Modern French Theatre*, ed. and trans. Michael Benedikt and George E. Wellwarth. New York: Dutton, 1964. Pp. 197–210.
Impromptu délibéré: Entretiens avec Paul-Louis Mignon. Paris: Gallimard, 1966.

Works of Salacrou's Critics

BOOKS DEVOTED ENTIRELY TO THE STUDY OF SALACROU'S THEATRE

Mignon, Paul-Louis. *Salacrou*. La Bibliothèque idéale. Paris: Gallimard, 1960. (Contains an extensive bibliography.)

Van Den Esch, José. *Armand Salacrou, dramaturge de l'angoisse*. Paris: Editions du Temps Présent, 1947.

BOOKS DEVOTED IN PART TO THE STUDY OF SALACROU'S THEATRE

Bourdet, Denise. *Pris sur le vif*. Paris: Librairie Plon, 1957.

Brodin, Pierre. *Présences contemporaines*. Paris: Nouvelles Editions Debresse, 1954.

Guicharnaud, Jacques. *Modern French Theatre*. New Haven, Conn.: Yale University Press, 1961.

Hobson, Harold. *The French Theatre of Today*. London: George G. Harrap and Co., 1953.

Jacquot, J., ed. *Le Théâtre moderne: Hommes et tendances*. Paris: Editions du Centre National de la Recherche Scientifique, 1958.

Kemp, Robert. *La Vie du théâtre*. Paris: Albin Michel, 1956.

Lumley, Frederick. *Trends in Twentieth-Century Drama*. London: Barrie and Rockliff, 1956.

Radine, Serge. *Anouilh, Lenormand, Salacrou: trois dramaturges à la recherche de leur vérité*. Genève: Editions des Trois Collines, 1951.

Sée, Edmond. *Le Théâtre français contemporain*. Paris: Armand Colin, 1950.

Simon, Pierre-Henri. *Théâtre et destin*. Paris: Armand Colin, 1959.

Sion, Georges. *Le Théâtre français d'entre-deux-guerres*. Tournai-Paris: Casterman, 1943.

ARTICLES AND ESSAYS

Benard, Pierre. "Armand Salacrou ou la passion de la fantaisie," *Les Lettres françaises*, No. 46 (10 mars 1945).

Bourdet, Denise. "Armand Salacrou," *La Revue de Paris*, 62e année (sept. 1955).

Charmel, André. "Essai sur le théâtre d'Armand Salacrou," *Europe*, 27e année, No. 37 (janvier 1949).

Delpech, Jeannine. "Le Théâtre d'aujourd'hui: Armand Salacrou," *Les Nouvelles littéraires*, No. 969 (28 février 1946).

Dubois, Jacques. "Entretien avec Armand Salacrou," *Les Lettres françaises*, 2e année, No. 439 (13–20 nov. 1952).

Fauve, Jacques. "A Drama of Essence: Salacrou and Others," *Yale French Studies*, No. 14 (Winter 1954–55).

24

Hahn, Paul. "Introducing Armand Salacrou," *Educational Theatre Journal*, III, No. 1 (March 1951).

Hombourger, René. "Ein Dramatiker: Armand Salacrou," *Antares*, IV. Jahrg., Nr. 4 (Juni 1956), Nr. 5 (Juli 1956).

Lusseyran, Jacques P. "La Malédiction de la solitude chez Anouilh et Salacrou," *French Review*, XXXIX, No. 3 (Dec. 1965).

Marcabru, Pierre. "Armand Salacrou: personnage de théâtre qui écrit pour le théâtre," *Paris-Théâtre*, 2e année, No. 122 (1957).

Poujol, Jacques. "Salacrou l'inquiéteur," *French Review*, XXVII, No. 6 (May 1954).

Silenieks, Juris. "Circularity of Plot in Salacrou's Plays," *Symposium*, XX, No. 1 (Spring 1966).

Vial, Fernand. "Montherlant and the Post-War Drama in France," *American Society Legion of Honor Magazine*, XXII, No. 1 (Spring 1951).

The World Is Round

(LA TERRE EST RONDE)

A PLAY IN THREE ACTS BY
ARMAND SALACROU

ENGLISH VERSION BY NORMAN STOKLE

Characters in Order of Their Appearance

MANENTE, a rich middle-aged pharmacist

FRA MARIANO, a Franciscan monk

GIACCOMO, an inexperienced young man

WOMAN, a courtesan

SILVIO, a charming young man

BARTHOLOMEO, a friend of Silvio

MARGHERITA, a widow in her forties, paid companion of Minutello's daughters

CLARISSA, a friend of Margherita, employed in Minutello's household

MINUTELLO, a rich wool merchant

LUCCIANA, Minutello's younger daughter

FAUSTINA, Minutello's elder daughter

UDERIGO, an astrologer

PEASANT, a servant in Minutello's household

BROTHER JEROME SAVONAROLA, a Dominican monk, prior of the Convent of San Marco

COGNAC, a young French soldier

FOUR CHILDREN   BUTCHER   EXECUTIONER

ACT I

Scene 1

Town square in Florence, 1492. It is carnival time. As the curtain rises, Manente, a middle-aged pharmacist, mask in hand, is in heated discussion with Fra Mariano, a Franciscan monk.

MANENTE. No, no, no. That's rubbish! You can't argue in 1492 as you did in 1482. How stupid can you be!

FRA MARIANO. But brother . . .

MANENTE. In ten years everything changes, sir. We progress.

FRA MARIANO. Yes indeed. Ten years ago, I was a young boy.

MANENTE. This is the age of enlightenment. We are no longer chained to the past. We live in the contemporary modern world . . .

FRA MARIANO. But . . .

MANENTE. . . . of today. Of 1492.

FRA MARIANO. (*timidly*) How do you mean?

MANENTE. (*exiting angrily*) Oooh!

FRA MARIANO. (*following him*) But my good Manente . . .

(*He exits. A young woman enters followed by Giaccomo. Both wear masks.*)

GIACCOMO. Sit down here beside me. (*She sits.*) Ah! Ah!

WOMAN. What is it?

GIACCOMO. Such exquisite buttocks! So rounded. So lovely. Molding themselves into new shapes on this stone. I wish I were this stone. Then I'd mold your body — with my hands. Oh to be my hands, nothing but my hands. Or your body. I wish I were your body. (*The Woman is horrified.*) My words move you deeply,

I can see that. I created them three years ago for a girl I knew, but she only laughed. She didn't understand. So they are still new, unused, always waiting ready on my lips. Now, I shall never say them again because you have understood them. I give them to you forever. (*sound of distant singing*) Do you hear Lorenzo's song?

WOMAN. Which Lorenzo?

GIACCOMO. Which Lorenzo! Has Florence more than one? Lorenzo the Magnificent, of course, the one true Lorenzo, our prince . . . Do you know him?

WOMAN. The Medici Lorenzo? Not likely.

GIACCOMO. What would you do if he came along here now and called out to you? Go off with him as you did with me?

WOMAN. You're a funny one.

GIACCOMO. Not funny, just modest. Why should you prefer me to Lorenzo of Medici?

WOMAN. Are we going to sit here long?

GIACCOMO. You were waiting for me, weren't you?

WOMAN. You . . . like all the rest.

GIACCOMO. What do you mean?

WOMAN. Don't we always wait for the one who comes?

GIACCOMO. Oh! What a philosophic mind.

WOMAN. Are you sure you know what I am?

GIACCOMO. I know you already like my soul, as a bee knows the rose . . . These sturdy legs did their best day's work when they led me to you. Will you kiss my leg too? My right leg?

WOMAN. I'll do anything you fancy.

GIACCOMO. Ah, what Heaven! Pure Heaven! If what I'm about to say shocks you, close your ears. Could you come back to my place . . . without feeling nervous?

WOMAN. Why should I feel nervous? It won't be the first time I've gone home with a fellow. Cost you more, that's all.

GIACCOMO. What do you mean?

WOMAN. Look, love, do you know me or don't you? I'm one of the girls from Canette Street. Know what I mean?

GIACCOMO. Oooh!

30

WOMAN. Well, what's got into you?

GIACCOMO. Oooh!

WOMAN. What are you bubbling about?

GIACCOMO. Oooooh!

WOMAN. I've told you, I don't mind going to your place.

GIACCOMO. Oh! Love, love, where are you?

WOMAN. I've told you. I'm willing.

GIACCOMO. (*sobbing*) But I don't feel like it any more.

WOMAN. Why ever not?

GIACCOMO. To be a tool of your trade!

WOMAN. Huh, don't flatter yourself, dearie! Besides, it's every woman's trade. You should know that.

GIACCOMO. If it wasn't me, it would be somebody else.

WOMAN. But since it is you . . .

GIACCOMO. Alas!

WOMAN. What's the difference if someone could take your place?

GIACCOMO. I wanted to conquer. To seduce.

WOMAN. Well, cheer up. I'm seduced.

(*Silvio and Bartholomeo enter.*)

SILVIO. Giaccomo!

GIACCOMO. Oh, my friends!

BARTHOLOMEO. What's all this? You crying?

WOMAN. He a friend of yours? Proper queer he is, I'll tell you. Proper queer.

(*Silvio and Bartholomeo look at each other and burst out laughing.*)

BARTHOLOMEO. Giaccomo!

SILVIO. Ssh! Here they come. On with the masks. (*to Giaccomo and Woman*) Quiet, you two.

(*Margherita, masked, and Dame Clarissa enter.*)

BARTHOLOMEO. (*to Clarissa*) Forgive my rudeness, reverent lady, but I have a word to ask of Dame Margherita. (*aside to Margherita*) Well?

MARGHERITA. No Faustina for you tonight.

BARTHOLOMEO. Why not?

31

MARGHERITA. Signore Minutello won't allow Lucciana and Faustina out of his sight on account of the carnival.

BARTHOLOMEO. What does Faustina say?

MARGHERITA. She's taken her father's moral advice to heart.

SILVIO. (*indignant*) Moral advice!

BARTHOLOMEO. Change nothing on our program, dear Margherita. Signore Minutello's daughters will be available tonight.

MARGHERITA. How so?

BARTHOLOMEO. Leave everything to me.

MARGHERITA. Well, in that case, I'll be available myself!

BARTHOLOMEO. We'll find you a partner, won't we, Giaccomo?

GIACCOMO. Eh? Oh, I er . . .

BARTHOLOMEO. (*to the Woman*) Come with us. I need you.

WOMAN. What for?

BARTHOLOMEO. Let's go, gentlemen. We also have advice to give — moral advice for the benefit of old men. (*to Dame Margherita*) Keep everything as planned, you gorgeous creature!

(*All exit, except Clarissa and Margherita.*)

CLARISSA. Dame Margherita, you should be ashamed of yourself — wearing a mask!

MARGHERITA. It's carnival day, isn't it?

CLARISSA. At your age!

MARGHERITA. That's why I wear the mask. If I were younger, I'd show my face.

CLARISSA. Exactly what I mean. At your age with all these young men! Have you no shame?

MARGHERITA. No, not at the moment. I'm having far too good a time.

CLARISSA. What about afterwards?

MARGHERITA. Afterwards, I'll confess to the priest.

CLARISSA. How you've changed since your poor husband died.

MARGHERITA. Why feel sorry for him? If he was as perfect as he said he was, he'll be in Heaven by now.

CLARISSA. How do you expect him to be in Heaven when he sees your debauched life on earth? Do you think that will make him happy?

32

MARGHERITA. If eternity's as long as they say, he won't mind me keeping him waiting a few years. I'll be up there to join him in a little while, then we'll go around Heaven arm in arm together.

CLARISSA. You'll end up in Hell.

MARGHERITA. After going to communion every morning? Don't you believe it. Anyhow, why reproach me — a lonely widow? You're all right. You have a husband.

CLARISSA. You don't imagine there's anything left in him, do you?

MARGHERITA. Maybe not, but you can still hope. Whereas I know my bed's empty.

CLARISSA. Do you think Signore Minutello will continue entrusting his two daughters to you when he finds out you cavort with every Tom, Dick, and Harry in Florence?

MARGHERITA. Goodbye, Clarissa. See you in church.

CLARISSA. Why should I go to church. I don't have sins to confess every day.

MARGHERITA. There are other kinds of sin, Clarissa. You only seem to think of the most agreeable kind. I wonder why? (*Clarissa exits. Margherita knocks at the door of Minutello's house.*) Yoo-hoo! It's me. Dame Margherita!

(*The scene opens onto the interior of Minutello's house. Minutello is talking to his two daughters, Faustina and Lucciana.*)

MINUTELLO. No, Faustina. That's final. You are not going to the ball tonight. I know best, don't I, Lucciana?

LUCCIANA. Yes, papa.

FAUSTINA. She likes church; I like dancing. You let her go to mass but stop me going to the ball. You are misinformed, papa. Nowadays, monks are more dangerous than dancers.

MINUTELLO. I know what those young men are after at the ball. At least in my day . . .

FAUSTINA. So, you went to the ball when you were our age?

MINUTELLO. That's precisely why I don't want my daughters to go.

FAUSTINA. Did you behave badly, papa?

MINUTELLO. Hush, child.

FAUSTINA. I heard you reminiscing once about those times. And you said, "Ah! Happy days, happy days!"

33

MINUTELLO. Girls must have self-respect, and respect their fathers and future husbands.

FAUSTINA. What could be the harm in my dancing with a handsome young man if I wanted to?

MINUTELLO. That's enough.

FAUSTINA. No, it's not. I want you to explain why the ball is dangerous — in detail.

MINUTELLO. I know what I'm talking about.

FAUSTINA. But what are you talking about?

MINUTELLO. Love! There must be no love outside of marriage. That's what I'm talking about, you minx.

FAUSTINA. Since mother died, you don't seem to love anyone anymore.

LUCCIANA. Faustina!

MINUTELLO. I will not give way to persuasion or insults, my girl. (*Enter Margherita.*) Greetings, Dame Margherita. As all the riffraff in Florence have the right to kiss every girl in sight on carnival day, you will wear these masks. As soon as you've called on my sister, you will immediately return here — keeping a firm hand on both my daughters all the way. You wear a mask too, Dame Margherita, and should you have any trouble with the young ruffians in the streets, remove yours, dear lady, and tell them you are the prettiest of the three.

(*Minutello's house disappears. We are now back in the square. Silvio and Bartholomeo enter.*)

SILVIO. Ha, Ha! Pull off such an idea and Faustina will be yours for more than just tonight.

BARTHOLOMEO. Let's get tonight over first.

SILVIO. What about tomorrow night?

BARTHOLOMEO. What is our existence but the addition of all our todays. When tomorrow comes, it changes its name and calls itself today. My friend, there's only one tomorrow, the one we'll never see. (*Fra Mariano, Manente, and Uderigo enter. To Fra Mariano*) Good brother, I should like to be as certain about my future life as you are about yours. Tell me, what is your fee for a place in Heaven?

FRA MARIANO. Quite the businessman, aren't you! Florence has so little demand for Heaven on carnival day, especially from lads your age. So, I'll give you a fair price. Stand us all a drink.

SILVIO. A drink? Good God! Heaven for a flagon of wine! Have you been there already to know that's all it's worth?

MANENTE. Here comes the king of the wool merchants with his two daughters.

(*Dame Margherita, Faustina, Lucciana, and Minutello enter.*)

UDERIGO. Fine looking girls they are too.

MANENTE. If only I were fifteen years younger!

SILVIO. Which one would you have?

MANENTE. I'd be quite happy with the one who wanted me.

BARTHOLOMEO. Greetings, my noble lord!

MINUTELLO. Out of the way, you ruffians. Off you go, my children. And Dame Margherita, return home before dark. (*The ladies exit.*) Bringing up two daughters is no easy job for a widower, I can tell you.

BARTHOLOMEO. Do they cause you much worry?

MINUTELLO. More than all the wool merchants in Florence, Bruges, and London put together.

SILVIO. Place them in our hands. We'll send them back with lots of experience.

MINUTELLO. Has it ever occurred to you that some day you may have daughters of your own?

BARTHOLOMEO. And don't you remember when you were twenty years old?

MANENTE. I'm not twenty and I have no daughters, but I ask you this: Which is more unbearable — to remember the twenty years you have already lived or to remember you can never live them over again?

SILVIO. But having lived them, aren't they still yours?

MANENTE. What of the great Lorenzo, our favorite son? The greatest of all the Medicis? He's not twenty anymore.

BARTHOLOMEO. He'll always seem twenty to me.

MANENTE. I took him some medicine this morning. And I tell you, he hasn't long to live.

BARTHOLOMEO. A fine pharmacist you are!

UDERIGO. There's no hope for Lorenzo of Medici, gentlemen. I have read his horoscope.

SILVIO. To hell with your stars!

UDERIGO. Ugh! Perhaps you don't realize, you ignorant young puppy, that there is not a bishop who would believe in the mission of Christ had we astrologers not confirmed it.

FRA MARIANO. Don't tell me there is some truth to Savonarola's prophecies after all. That raving old braggart predicted over a week ago Lorenzo would die. Now his prophecies are coming true.

UDERIGO. Some prophecy, I must say! Predicting the death of a dying man.

FRA MARIANO. What do your stars have to say about this unknown Dominican upstart?

MANENTE. Brother, don't upset yourself over that vomiting scoundrel.

FRA MARIANO. Preachers who can crack their voices with emotion are much in vogue these days.

MANENTE. Fashions don't last long in Florence.

FRA MARIANO. Which of us would have dared stand up in the cathedral and say, "Lorenzo, Prince of Florence, you will die for your sins"?

BARTHOLOMEO. That monk is just a vulgar loudmouth.

SILVIO. (*crossing himself*) Lorenzo, I shall believe in God so that you may be restored to health, and so that Ovid may be in Heaven with Socrates, Plato, Jesus, and our divine Homer.
(*A peasant enters.*)

PEASANT. None of your Homers could stop Lorenzo of Medici from calling in Brother Jerome to give him the last rites.

FRA MARIANO. What's this you say? Savonarola summoned by the Prince?

PEASANT. He's called our good Brother Jerome to the palace to give him absolution.

MANENTE. This new monk's prophecies must have really shaken him.

SILVIO. Lorenzo the Magnificent received me in his rooms this morning. He looked pale. I read him my poem and it appealed to him so much he gave me his finest dagger. (*shows it*) What a great prince! He enjoyed hearing me joke and sing even though he knew that death might strike him this very night.

PEASANT. Yes . . . go on.

SILVIO. And he sang me this song:

> How fair is youth, this golden day
> Which passes all too fleetingly.
> So let's make merry while we may
> Tomorrow we may never see.*

PEASANT. That's why he's called in Brother Jerome. So he can die well.

BARTHOLOMEO. No one ever dies well, you stupid bumpkin.

FRA MARIANO. The Prince of Florence is far too concerned with this little monk. Where he came from, Heaven only knows, but by the end of Lent, he'll have completely fizzled out, mark my words.

PEASANT. He's off to a good start, anyway. Six weeks ago, he was all alone. Now, there are more than a hundred of us behind him. I've heard him speak, and you know, he just laughs at all them books in Greek and Latin what I can't read. And he tells us about a Heaven that's real, just like my vines and my olive trees.

MANENTE. The Prince was wrong to send for Savonarola. It makes him look important.

BARTHOLOMEO. You're forgetting it's the carnival today. Sending for this Dominican is just another of Lorenzo's masks to show off in the streets of Florence, that's all.

UDERIGO. Let us not waste our time on this whining phrasemonger, this mob flatterer, this frothy-mouthed hypocrite.

GIACCOMO. It's always the same old cry: reform, be virtuous, be

*The words in the Italian original are:

> Quanto è bella Giovinezza
> Che si fugge tutta via
> Chi vuol esser lieto, sia.
> Di doman non c'è certezza.

moral. Oooh! He even goes without women! I ask you, were the best things in life created just to be thrown aside?

SILVIO. Lorenzo won't allow himself to die on carnival day. He's too considerate. Let's go and drink. We'll mourn for him tomorrow.

UDERIGO. Not a bad idea.

MANENTE. I agree.

BARTHOLOMEO. Signore Minutello.

MINUTELLO. What is it now?

BARTHOLOMEO. Silvio would like to talk with you.

MINUTELLO. Very long?

BARTHOLOMEO. Just a word.

MINUTELLO. (*to the others*) I'll be with you directly, gentlemen. (*They leave.*) Yes, Silvio?

SILVIO. My lord, you know Giaccomo?

MINUTELLO. Which one?

BARTHOLOMEO. Our Giaccomo.

MINUTELLO. The stupid one?

SILVIO. You, of all people, have no right to laugh at him. Not anymore.

MINUTELLO. No right, at my age, to laugh at a little urchin like him?

BARTHOLOMEO. He's very unhappy, thanks to you.

MINUTELLO. Me?

BARTHOLOMEO. A dying man, and it's all your fault.

MINUTELLO. What the devil is all this?

SILVIO. Poor Giaccomo! He's fallen madly in love with this woman. But when they are together, all she does is pine for you. "I love only Signore Minutello," she says.

MINUTELLO. What! Already a matchmaker, and you from such a good family!

SILVIO. No one asked me to tell you. It's just that the delightful young creature came to me and cried her heart out, all the while calling your name.

BARTHOLOMEO. And Giaccomo cried his heart out to me, only he kept calling your name, too.

38

MINUTELLO. Are you trying to palm me off onto some out-of-work tart, by any chance? Or some lame old hag?

BARTHOLOMEO. She's married but her husband travels a lot.

MINUTELLO. I can well imagine the type she is.

SILVIO. Look. (*shows her portrait*) My distinguished friend Botticelli painted her as a madonna.

MINUTELLO. Mm! Very nice. I say it in all good faith. She really is quite lovely, I must say. But how could this woman possibly be in love with me?

SILVIO. Don't you believe in the miracles of the Holy Church?

BARTHOLOMEO. But we must tell you the whole story. She is closely watched by a vicious mother-in-law.

MINUTELLO. Ah! Now I understand, you rogues. I have to climb high walls and be frightened out of my wits by bloodhounds before I can reach her. Then I end up getting locked in some closet or other. A fine fool I'd look when my friends heard about that.

BARTHOLOMEO. No, Signore Minutello. Tonight, she'll be coming to this very square to look up at your windows. And she's much prettier than that old crow you meet in the hay at the back of your stables every morning.

MINUTELLO. What the devil do you mean, you evil-minded monkey?

BARTHOLOMEO. It's the talk of the town.

SILVIO. Now don't let it go to your head. She's in love with you but you'll have certain barriers to break down. With her honor to the right and her burning desire to the left, there's a violent summer storm brewing in her young maiden heart.

MINUTELLO. (*suspiciously*) But you told me she was married.

SILVIO. Just for three days. Then her husband had to leave for Leghorn and sail to Greece. We did everything we could to console her, believe me. But alas, young men bore her and the only thing she enjoys is talking to mature men with power and stature.

MINUTELLO. And money?

BARTHOLOMEO. I've yet to meet a woman in Florence who'd turn her nose up at money. The richest of them make you bribe their servants into silence and afterwards collect half the purse.

39

SILVIO. But this charming girl will cost only what you give her.

MINUTELLO. That's what I like to hear, Silvio. Just what I give her, and by temperament, I'm very thrifty.

BARTHOLOMEO. Play it gently the first time. She loves you. Don't abuse it.

MINUTELLO. I know what to do, you little idiot. I wooed women before you were born and when I feel like it, I seduce.

SILVIO. Quiet, you seducer! Here she comes.

BARTHOLOMEO. Don't go about it like some stupid monk.

SILVIO. Talk to her a little before trying to rape her. (*A masked woman enters wearing the same coat as the woman seen before.*) This is my lord Minutello, dear lady.

(*The two young men go off. A silence follows.*)

WOMAN. Sir . . .

(*There is a silence.*)

MINUTELLO. Madam. (*a silence*) Madam . . . I . . . (*The Woman sighs.*) Please don't think I'm ignorant of how to address a lady. Is it really me you wish to see?

WOMAN. Yes.

MINUTELLO. I can hardly believe my luck.

WOMAN. What luck?

MINUTELLO. Then was Silvio lying when he said you loved me?

WOMAN. You don't even know me. How can you be so excited just because a woman you've never even seen before happens to love you? Doesn't it matter who she is?

MINUTELLO. I know you're pretty.

WOMAN. Is that enough?

MINUTELLO. I also know your husband is far away.

WOMAN. Perhaps so, but I still can't marry you.

MINUTELLO. Who's talking about marriage? Silvio only mentioned love.

WOMAN. Shouldn't a woman think first of her honor?

MINUTELLO. When you're as old as I am and have spent all your life talking about honor, maybe you'll be sorry you didn't talk about love a bit more.

WOMAN. What of Hell's damnation?

MINUTELLO. Looking at you, I lose all fear of Hell.

WOMAN. It's so sinful.

MINUTELLO. At the moment, I find it delicious.

WOMAN. I'm afraid.

MINUTELLO. But they told me your husband was miles away.

WOMAN. That doesn't worry me. It's just that my father told me not to love anyone outside of marriage.

MINUTELLO. I know a very understanding Franciscan friar. He'll arrange everything.

WOMAN. How?

MINUTELLO. He will marry us — in his own little way.

WOMAN. What will I do when my husband returns?

MINUTELLO. You're a Florentine woman, aren't you? You should know how to hush things up.

WOMAN. Will the Holy Virgin not blush with shame seeing us together?

MINUTELLO. She can always look the other way.

WOMAN. I wish my father could hear you.

MINUTELLO. Why?

WOMAN. Because he'd be able to answer you. And I'd be very interested to hear what you'd say to each other.

MINUTELLO. I'd tell him . . . er . . . well . . . I'd tell him a father should not concern himself anymore with a married daughter. I'd tell him he's very lucky to have her married off and should thank Heaven for being relieved of his responsibilities.

WOMAN. Does a father stop loving his daughter once she is married?

MINUTELLO. I don't mean that. But your loving me is nobody's concern except your husband's.

WOMAN. Should I tell him about it, do you think?

MINUTELLO. What! Are you stupid?

WOMAN. I don't know. But they say a woman always appears a little stupid to the man she refuses.

MINUTELLO. Why refuse yourself if you love me?

WOMAN. I'm afraid.

MINUTELLO. What is there to be afraid of? My house has thick walls. You can come there secretly tonight, and together in my room, just the two of us, we'll enjoy being alive.

WOMAN. And tomorrow, I shall be tired. My father will be shocked seeing me so pale and listless. He'll call the doctor. He'll start worrying.

MINUTELLO. Ah! What a charming girl. If only I had daughters who'd refuse themselves like you, out of respect and affection for their father.

WOMAN. You have shown me the path of virtue. Goodbye, my sweet lord.

MINUTELLO. Are you insane? After such fine sentiments and glowing tributes to your family's reputation, your conscience must surely be satisfied. (*sound of music*) Listen to the songs of Florence. Come to my arms. I'll make you rich.

WOMAN. You will give me money?

MINUTELLO. Yes, and much more than I ever dreamed possible.

WOMAN. No closer, please. I'd rather not come to your house the first time. Wait for me in the park tonight at ten.

MINUTELLO. I'm past the stage of waiting for a woman under a tree. Come to my house.

WOMAN. No.

MINUTELLO. Why not?

WOMAN. Suppose I bumped into your daughters? They know me.

MINUTELLO. Oh, very well. I'll pack them off to the ball.

WOMAN. Good. Then I'll come. But you must tell them to come back late. Very late . . .

MINUTELLO. No, I'd better keep them at home. I'll send a carriage to pick you up and we'll go over to Fiesole.

WOMAN. Fiesole? It's full of witches. Besides, it's too far.

MINUTELLO. Don't torture me like this. I'll give you all the money you want. I feel your youth; I know you're beautiful. I saw your picture. I'm not young any more. And you love me. They said you were weeping because of me. You are the last woman I'll ever love. When you go, there'll be nothing left in my life except to wait for death. If you only knew how difficult it is for me to

42

resign myself to old age. But now, with you, I'm going to live again.

WOMAN. Please stop. Listen. I didn't want to come but Bartholomeo and Silvio forced me into it. And I agreed because I thought we'd only arrange to meet in the park. But things have gone too far. I'm sorry. Please forgive me and let me go.

MINUTELLO. Stay. I beg you. I'll give you anything you ask if only you will love me. I'll give you anything you ask even if you don't love me, but please stay near me.

(*Bartholomeo and Silvio enter. They call in a whisper.*)

SILVIO. Manente!

BARTHOLOMEO. Uderigo. Giaccomo!

(*Uderigo and Giaccomo enter followed by Fra Mariano.*)

SILVIO. Fra Mariano will bless this marriage.

WOMAN. (*to Bartholomeo*) If you love me, let me leave wearing the mask.

MINUTELLO. She is a respectable lady. You will not touch her mask.

SILVIO. But which is her mask? (*He pulls off her mask. It is Faustina, Minutello's eldest daughter. Showing the mask*) This? (*pointing to her face*) or that? (*laughs*)

MANENTE. You young fellows are too cruel.

MINUTELLO. Faustina!

FRA MARIANO. Making advances to your own daughter, indeed! Where do you think you are? In the papal court?

FAUSTINA. (*to Bartholomeo*) Take me away. I'm so ashamed.

BARTHOLOMEO. Ashamed? You?

FAUSTINA. Yes, I feel sick with myself.

(*Faustina and Bartholomeo exit.*)

MINUTELLO. Can my own daughter be such a hussy?

SILVIO. If she'd been someone else's daughter, the hussy might have been very much to your liking.

MINUTELLO. Silvio! Silvio! If you live to be my age, the memory of this day will eat out your heart.

SILVIO. Would you have held back if she had been my sister? Why should a man of your age have two moral codes? One for your own daughters and another for someone else's?

MANENTE. (*to Fra Mariano and Uderigo*) Let us never mention this business again to our good neighbor.

MINUTELLO. Mark my words, Silvio. If God is just, he will curse you for this. (*exits*)

GIACCOMO. How do you feel?

SILVIO. What about?

GIACCOMO. Being cursed.

SILVIO. Look, Giaccomo. I curse you. Now, how do you feel?

GIACCOMO. That's all very well, but he was in tears.

SILVIO. Oh, get the hell out of here. Go on, or I'll curse you again. (*All have exited. Enter Lucciana and Margherita.*)

LUCCIANA. My father gave Faustina to your charge. Why did you let her out of your sight? She's been gone an hour.

MARGHERITA. (*very worried*) She'll be back, don't worry.

LUCCIANA. And father's so nervous about us being out.

MARGHERITA. She promised to meet us at the Baptistry by three. She's a sensible girl, your sister. When I give her such freedom she invariably comes back on time.

LUCCIANA. To begin with, where did she go?

MARGHERITA. I don't know.

LUCCIANA. You know perfectly well.

SILVIO. (*entering masked*) A kiss, carnival rights!

MARGHERITA. Out of my way, you lout.

SILVIO. Carnival rights. A kiss to pass.

MARGHERITA. Give it to me, then.

SILVIO. What a glutton for sex! Silvio greets you. (*takes off his mask*)

MARGHERITA. Tell me, Silvio, where is Faustina?

SILVIO. Brother Jerome predicts the future, so he knows where she'll be tomorrow. But as for the present, who can say? Ah, Dame Margherita, in this world, two things are simple: to tell the past and predict the future. But to see clearly from one day to the next, that's another matter.

LUCCIANA. Let's go home, Dame Margherita.

MARGHERITA. Without Faustina? What will I tell your father?

SILVIO. Better hurry. She's waiting for you outside the inn by the new bridge.

MARGHERITA. Come, Lucciana.

SILVIO. Go alone. Giaccomo is there too. He wants a word with you in private about tonight.

MARGHERITA. Giaccomo! Holy Virgin! I must go. Protect this child! Wait for me here, Lucciana. Don't move from this spot. I'll be back with your sister before you can say Jack Robinson. (*scuttles off*)

LUCCIANA. Let me pass.

SILVIO. Not so fast. I must obey the carnival rites. Faustina tells me you have torn up all my poems.

LUCCIANA. Yes.

SILVIO. But you read them first. Lucciana, you looked at me three times during mass on Sunday.

LUCCIANA. That's not true. Let me pass.

SILVIO. (*putting on mask*) Carnival rights, Lucciana. A kiss for letting you pass.

LUCCIANA. No.

SILVIO. I've the right to steal one from you.

LUCCIANA. How much would a stolen kiss be worth?

SILVIO. Stolen fruit always tastes sweetest.

LUCCIANA. You brute!

SILVIO. (*taking off mask*) Who, me?

LUCCIANA. Where is your conscience?

SILVIO. Who has a conscience at twenty . . . or when he's rich? If I overwork my conscience now, what will I have to keep me busy in my old age?

LUCCIANA. You lecherous monster!

SILVIO. Tut tut! Contaminating the air of Florence with such language.

LUCCIANA. What can my sister be doing? Where is Faustina?

SILVIO. She told me you called out my name in your dreams. Silvio! Silvio!

LUCCIANA. It was she who was dreaming.

(*Silvio tries to kiss her; she grabs his dagger.*)

SILVIO. Lucciana . . .

LUCCIANA. (*pulling away from him*) Take care! I have your dagger!

45

SILVIO. (*laughing*) To kill me with?

LUCCIANA. No. Come to me now if you like. But I warn you, Silvio, the closer you come, the closer this blade will be to my heart. No more kisses? Come. I love you, Silvio. Now I can tell you since I am going to die.

SILVIO. You love me?

LUCCIANA. Yes, and with your dagger at my breast, I'm asking you to kiss me, Silvio.

SILVIO. I can't do it. I can't do it. See you tomorrow, Lucciana.

LUCCIANA. Don't forget your knife.

SILVIO. Keep it. May it protect you as well from other men.

LUCCIANA. Won't you exchange my death for a kiss? Do you love me a little, then, Silvio?

SILVIO. Goodbye, Lucciana. (*exits*)

LUCCIANA. Silvio . . . How do you know I would have killed myself?

Scene 2

The cell of Brother Jerome Savonarola. He is alone.

JEROME. I am prior of Saint Mark's. My convent, in the midst of this decadent city, is sorely troubled.

Human utterance is but a string of syllables. While one yet lives, the others have already become as nothing. So much for our human utterance. Only the word of God is eternal. I shall speak that word. Oh Florence, you corrupted city . . . No, no, no. My time has not yet arrived.

This morning, a Florentine woman gave a small casket of beeswax to Saint Francis as a votive offering. Why? Because her lover, a monk, had consumed an entire barrel of wine without her husband noticing the theft. Such is the function of our monks, our churches, and our saints. The soul of Florence is cankerous.

Oh women, I live without sin. I have sacrificed everything for Christ, even my own mother. And today, that same Christ stands deserted in our churches while you, you glorify your bodies with

46

trinkets and perfumes. You dye your hair, you paint your fingers. But you are ugly, and you smell of sin. What was that? You go to church on Sundays? What of the other days? Does God sleep from Monday till Saturday? The world is flowing with blood, but the priests no longer comfort our troubled minds. Nowadays, their religion is fornication. They gossip all day in the choir of their churches and spend their nights with prostitutes. The high altar has become a business place for the priests. All things can be bought or sold. Women, bishoprics, even the rock of Saint Peter which now supports the buttocks of a Borgia. And Borgia is making the church in his own image. Those who can read devour lewd stories and those who can't read tell worse ones. I shall burn the books! I shall make men silent! I am your soldier, my Lord. I love my brothers and sisters because they are your creatures. Else when I looked at them, I should vomit.

Oh my God, I am good, but you wish me to be cruel. I was born to love, yet you tell me to punish, I who am alone against the world. My only desire was to stay alone on a mountain apart from other men, so much does their baseness revolt me. Help me, God; Satan will try to make me insane. Lord, I share your shame before the sins of your creatures. Forsake me not, then at the next carnival, men will no longer assault young girls but will sing hymns in your praise and the girls will be in my convents.

How shall I place them all in convents? How shall I make men sing to your glory? Rich and poor alike are against me, both consumed with corruption, and the rich with the added corruption of money. But I shall fight you. May the curse of God and Savonarola smite the affluent while children die of hunger. Possessing earthly riches is just as detestable as possessing a woman — though perhaps less sordid.

See my poverty, oh Lord. See my dedication to your glory and help me. For I am but a lowly man in a strange city, and you wish me to rise against your cardinals and generals.

First, I must break the power of the Medicis. I prophesied Lorenzo's death and he is dying, thanks be to God. But why did he call me to his deathbed? Are men so frightened of death? He committed his first political mistake in calling me. Surely he knew I was an enemy of his family. How could he hope I should give him absolution? On Sunday, in the cathedral, I shall explain why he summoned me, and why I condemned him. Then no longer shall I be just an ordinary monk, but one who refused absolution to the Prince of Florence.

As for Piero, that halfwit son of his, he thinks only of horses and women, boxing and books. Hear me well, son of Lorenzo, even your alliance with the corrupted Holy Church will not save you from my anathema.

What is this hand, with this sword, filling the sky? And this thunder? The sword turns towards the earth. All grows dark. I see no more. What means this hail of swords and arrows? Famine, plague, war. My poor Italy, what pestilence . . . this army of savages from the north led by the King of France. They plunder Rome . . . Oh God, why choose me to make such prophecies? That Charles VIII of France will invade Italy to punish her for her sins?

I clearly heard your voice. But why this thunder? Was I the only one on whom your eyes could rest? Why reserve so perilous a life for me? Why me? Savonarola was a simple peasant's name. Why make it the symbol of your bloodstained sword? Forgive me, my Lord, for having resisted you. I submit to your will.

Sin makes man unhappy. I shall reform man. I shall save him from Hell. I shall save Italy, my country, and make her strong and united. With your light upon me, Lord, I shall go forward to my brothers. By your command, I shall lead them to the Paradise they see reflected in my countenance. Amen.

Scene 3

Nighttime in front of Minutello's house. Dame Margherita is alone and on the lookout.

MARGHERITA. Here I am left outside while Lucciana and Silvio make up to each other, and me an old woman. At least I feel old when

I'm on my feet. I must keep a lookout for the master coming home. Oh, what with all that scandal over Faustina, he was wrong to keep me in his service. Very wrong. I don't deserve his confidence. No, indeed I don't.

Scene 4

Two months later. Lucciana's room.

LUCCIANA. My mind is made up, Silvio. We shall never see each other again.

SILVIO. Why tell me now, my sweet Lucciana? Would you have me treat this last evening as it deserves?

LUCCIANA. Yet I am not sure I can live through another day knowing all is ended between us.

SILVIO. Considering this our last meeting, I find your conversation quite delightful.

LUCCIANA. When I talk to you, I can't lie.

SILVIO. Why are you breaking with me?

LUCCIANA. My father won't even hear mention of your name.

SILVIO. Could he ever forgive me, do you think?

LUCCIANA. I hoped you might go to him on your knees and say, "Sir, I love Lucciana, and I'm bitterly sorry for being so stupid."

SILVIO. But I'm not sorry.

LUCCIANA. Why don't you ever say what your heart feels? Wasn't it your fault Faustina ran off to Rome where Heaven only knows what she is doing?

SILVIO. She's a cardinal's mistress. Heaven ought to know.

LUCCIANA. Well, I will not be Silvio's mistress.

SILVIO. Haven't I always behaved well towards you and been the most timid of fiancés?

LUCCIANA. How can you be my fiancé when you have no wish to be my husband?

SILVIO. Can't we just be good friends?

LUCCIANA. With you in my bedroom every night? I should never have let you come here in the first place. I should never have become accustomed to such happiness.

SILVIO. (*drinking*) And I've got used to having a glass of your father's wine before going to bed every night. Excellent wine it is, too.

LUCCIANA. It's so easy to make fun of everything. Why not try and make up your mind about things and give respect where it is due?

SILVIO. I respected Lorenzo while he was alive. May he now be in Heaven and I'll respect my promise to Lucciana.

LUCCIANA. Oh, it's all right for you men.

SILVIO. Someday when you're no longer a virgin and still remember me, ask your lovers if it was very easy for me to come to your room night after night and stay as well behaved as every priest should be.

LUCCIANA. Can you sleep after you've left me?

SILVIO. I try — so that I can dream about you.

LUCCIANA. Kiss me.

SILVIO. No.

LUCCIANA. Kiss me, Silvio.

SILVIO. You would throw me out afterwards.

LUCCIANA. But you would like to kiss me, wouldn't you?

SILVIO. Yes.

LUCCIANA. You do know how to kiss well, it's true. You must have known many other women before me.

SILVIO. You think so? I can't remember anymore.

LUCCIANA. Can one forget such things?

SILVIO. I suppose so.

LUCCIANA. Then if you were to kiss me tonight, could you forget all about it afterwards?

SILVIO. Who knows? Perhaps in later years a man is more likely to remember the kisses he never gave. You see, your role is the more beautiful because I shall not kiss you.

LUCCIANA. Do you enjoy watching a girl struggling within herself so much that you make no move to take her? Why do you force me into giving myself when I have no wish to be taken?

SILVIO. If your father asked Fra Mariano to marry us within the

50

sound of church bells, that would suit you beautifully, wouldn't it? Listen, Lucciana, ever since I started coming here at night, you know I have always forbidden you to confess to Fra Mariano. Well, I've changed my mind. Tomorrow morning, go and confess. Tell him you are torturing yourself with a secret scandalous love. Tell him you love a monk. Tell him the monk is called Fra Mariano — and I'll be burned alive in the city square if he is not in your room the same night like an oversexed rabbit introducing you to the finer points of love. He'll say he's a heavenly dove. While he's seducing you, he'll tell you all about the Holy Visitation. And that's the kind of man you want to bless our love and set your mind at rest.

LUCCIANA. What can I do? Here I am, alone, between you who refuse to understand me and my father who hates you. Holy Virgin, help me.

SILVIO. There's an idea. Do what she did. Marry a Joseph your father approves of and Silvio will be your heavenly dove.

LUCCIANA. Your blasphemies are so wicked, even Brother Jerome wouldn't believe them.

SILVIO. May the plague strike him dead.

LUCCIANA. But Silvio, he really is a virtuous monk.

SILVIO. Does he trouble your conscience?

LUCCIANA. Hasn't my love even helped you to save your own soul? Then I thank my father for being so stubborn. Because he spares me the certainty of knowing you refuse to marry me.

SILVIO. Stop talking like a child. You know nothing about life, so don't complain. I'm twenty-three. I have lived. And I know people aren't getting married anymore — especially since this morning.

LUCCIANA. Why this morning?

SILVIO. I've heard the most extraordinary thing, Lucciana. They say the world is round.

LUCCIANA. Which world?

SILVIO. Our world.

LUCCIANA. I don't understand.

SILVIO. Beyond Florence, there is Fiesole, Monte Cassino, the corrupt city of Pisa, and then the barbarian uncivilized countries and vast, mysterious seas. Well, they are all just one single ball in the sky.

LUCCIANA. Is this a riddle?

SILVIO. No. Listen. Explorers have put to sea from the south of Spain towards the setting sun. They will keep going straight ahead at full sail, always straight ahead, and then one day, their sails will appear among the Grecian islands.

LUCCIANA. It's stumped me. I give in.

SILVIO. How can I make you understand? Vespucci knows all about it. He was the one who told me.

LUCCIANA. That old drunkard?

SILVIO. No. His nephew, Amerigo. He wants to set sail too. In fact, he's leaving Florence the day after tomorrow and we've arranged to meet in Seville.

LUCCIANA. But you are not going?

SILVIO. With Amerigo, maybe.

LUCCIANA. So this is how you love me!

SILVIO. Why can't I love you just as well on the other side of the world?

LUCCIANA. But Silvio, there isn't any other side. And even if there were, it would be underneath and you'd fall off.

SILVIO. I don't think so.

LUCCIANA. Which way are you going?

SILVIO. We'll look at the stars and they will tell us.

LUCCIANA. But you always told me you didn't believe in the stars.

SILVIO. I do now.

LUCCIANA. You do? Then so do I. But Silvio, I ask you to love me in a way I can tell father about, and all you can say is Italy is an orange in the sky!

SILVIO. No. Not Italy. The whole world.

LUCCIANA. The whole world, then. And that you won't marry me because the world is round. Silvio, be reasonable.

SILVIO. I want to discover the whole world with my love brimming over for you. And out there in the deep oceans, I want to tell myself, I loved Lucciana as a pure sister. Then when I return, I shall be famous, having loved you and discovered the world.

LUCCIANA. Why do you want to be famous?

SILVIO. Isn't it pleasant to know you'll be admired centuries after you are dead?

LUCCIANA. Admired by people who aren't even born yet? Who aren't even little babies? That's ridiculous!

SILVIO. If you only knew the admiration we have today for Virgil or Hannibal or Alexander.

LUCCIANA. Are centuries of future reputation worth one day of happiness in the present?

MARGHERITA. (*entering*) Look out.

SILVIO. What is it?

MARGHERITA. Look out.

SILVIO. Are you drunk again?

MARGHERITA. With emotion. The old man is here.

LUCCIANA. Poor father!

SILVIO. Have you a balcony anywhere? A cupboard? Or a trunk?

LUCCIANA. (*indicating cupboard*) In here.

SILVIO. Oh, my wine.

MARGHERITA. Your father's on my heels.

SILVIO. Make yourself scarce. Don't look as though you'd forewarned us. Go on. Off with you!

(*He hides. Margherita goes off. Minutello enters.*)

MINUTELLO. Good evening, my dear. (*sits*) I'm so tired. They were all talking at once and I couldn't listen any longer. My only wish was to come and bid you good night. So I left before the end. Lucciana, I'm rich and I'm bored. The last days of my life have been the heaviest. To make matters worse, every family in Florence will be forced to take sides. Now, with the monk giving all the orders, what peace can there be for us anymore unless we're friends of his? I would have liked to be on good terms with everyone. But that's no longer possible. Now, one must be either for or against. I tried to calm them a little and do you know what Montefeltro said, my friend since childhood? Marino Minutello, he said, how can you remain unmoved by Brother Jerome who

denounces the corruption of Rome, when your daughter Faustina
is the prostitute of a cardinal?

LUCCIANA. Papa!

MINUTELLO. I left without a word. And thank goodness I did, because now I am here with you, with someone I can talk to. You
know I often think about Faustina. My associate in Rome
went to see her for me, and wrote me a letter. Brother Jerome is
right. There is corruption in Rome, and that corruption is my
daughter!

LUCCIANA. Papa!

MINUTELLO. She's covered with jewels. She has breakfast at the
Holy Father's table. And that's not all. I have other troubles.
Wool isn't selling any more. The market is bad. The men are
out of work. I know full well they have a right to eat just like
anybody else — but how do they expect me to keep them employed when I can't get any sale for my wool? And that's not the
end of it, either. Brother Jerome has prophesied a barbarian in-
vasion to punish Italy for her sins.

LUCCIANA. Which barbarians?

MINUTELLO. The French.

LUCCIANA. Heaven protect us.

MINUTELLO. I'm sorry for talking to you this way. As if you were
a man. But what else can I do? I have no sons. Well, goodnight, my dear. I've kept you a little late. You are tired. But,
now I think of it, why weren't you in bed when I came in?

LUCCIANA. I was reading, father.

MINUTELLO. You read too much. All these novels just turn your
head. Why on earth do you read stories about people you don't
know?

LUCCIANA. I'm not learned enough to describe the pleasure I derive
from reading, papa.

MINUTELLO. Stories that sometimes aren't even true?

LUCCIANA. They could be.

MINUTELLO. So you are bored too — needing other worlds to read
about? Tell me the story you were reading . . .

LUCCIANA. It's very long, father.

MINUTELLO. Never mind. Tell it to me.

LUCCIANA. It's about a very sweet girl who is very unhappy.

MINUTELLO. And very beautiful, of course . . .

LUCCIANA. I don't know.

MINUTELLO. What do you mean? You don't know?

LUCCIANA. She is in love with a handsome young man.

MINUTELLO. That's why I don't want you to read any more novels.

LUCCIANA. A man who is good and upright yet doesn't know it himself.

MINUTELLO. How so?

LUCCIANA. But she knows. And since she is as good and upright as he is and dearly loves him, she wants to become his wife.

MINUTELLO. Then why doesn't she marry him?

LUCCIANA. In spite of the boy's reluctance to settle down, he might perhaps be persuaded, but the girl's father will not hear of such a marriage.

MINUTELLO. Why not? Don't tell me your novel depicts the father as an imbecile?

LUCCIANA. No. But this young man has behaved very badly towards the father.

MINUTELLO. In what way?

LUCCIANA. He . . . er . . . he beat him.

MINUTELLO. He beat his future father-in-law?

LUCCIANA. At the time, he didn't know he would fall in love with this girl and she with him. It's such a sad story, papa. This girl was as pure as snow, and yet she would let the young man come up to her room.

MINUTELLO. Once and for all, you will read no more of these novels, my girl.

LUCCIANA. What else could she do?

MINUTELLO. But . . . but . . .

LUCCIANA. To safeguard her happiness, this poor girl had to run great risks. And I promise you, papa, when you know all the details of the story, that this young girl was very courageous. One night, the father suddenly enters the girl's room. She hides her sweetheart in a cupboard, prostrates herself before her father and says, "Father, if you will only let him see you, if only you will forgive him, the young man will come out of the cupboard, throw himself at your feet and we will be happily married."

MINUTELLO. The ending is better.

LUCCIANA. "You have no sons. You no longer have a wife. Your last-remaining possession is your daughter who loves you. You are bored with life. Your daughter sincerely wants to make you happy in your old age and give you grandchildren to climb up on your knee."

MINUTELLO. And then?

LUCCIANA. Then what?

MINUTELLO. What happened after that?

LUCCIANA. The father, who was just like you, started to weep.

MINUTELLO. Yes . . . ?

LUCCIANA. That's as far as I had read when you came in, papa.

MINUTELLO. Well, I know how it ends already. The father gets up, wipes away his tears, kisses his daughter, opens the cupboard and says, "My dear son-in-law, embrace me."

LUCCIANA. Dear, dear papa. How I do love you.

MINUTELLO. You see. I could have written novels myself if I'd felt like it. And just as well as anybody else. But I don't want you to read them any more. They falsify the mind. If I came into your room just now and found a man I heartily detested in your cupboard, do you think I should embrace him?

LUCCIANA. Then what would you do?

MINUTELLO. I should kill him with my sword. Where is my sword?

LUCCIANA. But papa, you are dreaming.

MINUTELLO. Now your novel is turning my head. What is the good of giving yourself to such imaginings and fanciful pictures? Come now. Goodnight, my little one. Say your prayers and go to sleep. I'll see you in the morning. (*exits*)

LUCCIANA. (*prays, then stops*) Silvio!

(*Silvio emerges from the cupboard.*)

LUCCIANA. Silvio! In all Heaven and earth, you are my only love. Silvio.

CURTAIN

56

ACT II

Scene 1

The living room in Minutello's house a few months later. The French army is now in Florence. Cognac, a young French soldier, has been billeted in Minutello's house. He speaks with a strong accent.

MARGHERITA. Drink up, dearest.

COGNAC. I no want drink.

MARGHERITA. A little Bologna, then?

COGNAC. I no like it.

MARGHERITA. Want anything else?

COGNAC. I 'ave not 'unger.

MARGHERITA. My handsome Frenchman, tell me, why is your king a hunchback?

COGNAC. Ze king? Is 'unchback? C'est possible, but I sought 'unchbacks zey bring good luck?

MARGHERITA. Aren't you happy here?

COGNAC. I am so tired.

MARGHERITA. Would you like to rest in your room?

COGNAC. I would like very much, but 'ow can I rest when we share ze same bed? Oh, mon dieu, what a war!

MARGHERITA. Is it true what they are saying about your king? That he can't even write his own name?

COGNAC. Do you sink we are all priests? And you always sink you are so clever, you know 'ow to write, I suppose, huh?

MARGHERITA. Then how do people in France keep their household accounts?

COGNAC. Can you write? (*laughs*)

MARGHERITA. Look, here's a letter I was writing to you. A real love letter, my angel.

COGNAC. (*suspiciously*) Who says zat's writing?

MARGHERITA. Can't you read either?

COGNAC. If you find me so stupid, give me back ze key to ze bedroom.

MARGHERITA. All right. Don't get upset. You know, Charles the Eighth is a funny name for a king. Is Eighth his surname?

COGNAC. (*laughing*) Eighz? His surname! Ha! Lot of good it does you knowing 'ow to read.

MARGHERITA. What is his surname, then?

COGNAC. His surname? Oh . . . bougre de bougre! You sink I come to make war in Italy just to tell you ze surname of our king?

MARGHERITA. Don't you know it? You're a funny one. Here in Florence it used to be the Medicis.

COGNAC. (*crying*) Oh, mon dieu, what a war.

MARGHERITA. Why are you crying? My handsome barbarian, aren't you happy here? We welcome your King Charles under a golden dias. We throw roses as your soldiers go by. What is there to cry about?

COGNAC. If you sink I leave France to get some stinking flowers srown in my face, you're crazy.

MARGHERITA. Would you rather have been run through with a sword?

COGNAC. Who said anysing about zat? If anybody get killed, I do it. A war of conquest, voilà! Zis is what I want. But you are a sly lot. And your monk, he is ze most sly. We 'ave to live wiz ze natives and no spitting on ze carpets. Zey say to be nice wiz ze ladies.

MARGHERITA. But you are nice, my love. Very nice.

COGNAC. Zis war, it is a crook. Zey are all crooks.

MARGHERITA. Us? Crooks?

COGNAC. Parfaitement! When ze seigneur of ze village call us togezer, he tell us — and me ze first — "Cognac," he say, "our great Charles goes to conquer ze Kingdom of Naples what belongs to him. And zen he go to Jerusalem to free ze tomb of ze Christ. Ze son of ze Holy Virgin. I must join him wiz twenty men," he say. "You come wiz me." "Me?" I say. "Leave home?" "Cognac," he say, "you are young. You will see ze world and 'ave a good time. We will kill ze old people for zeir jewels and whip ze young ones to show zem what is what. And when we take ze towns, zen we take ze women." Ha! Big joke! "Come ze night," he say, "we will burn ze whole cabboodle to light up ze dark. Zere will be old people wiz zeir guts hanging out. Zere will be beautiful girls in zeir nightshirts — all virgins. But zey will run away. We catch zem by ze arm and make ze cushions out of zem bobbing up and down on ze ground. Zen next day, we oop and start all over again. And like zis we go to Naples, zen Jerusalem to rescue ze Lord." Ha! Big deal! Look what happens. Here we are, received wiz flowers. If we bat an eyelid, we are 'anged by ze order of ze king. We live wiz ze natives and zey laugh at us because we don't know 'ow to read. And every night you are in my room. You don't let me sleep. And I want to sleep if only to dream I am still at home in France.

MARGHERITA. Didn't you slaughter everyone at Rapallo two months ago when you first came to Italy? Even the patients in the hospital? We all trembled in Florence when we heard about it. How when every living thing had been killed, you stuck your swords in the dead bodies, just to keep in practice.

COGNAC. Yes, but me, I am in ze artillery. I was back wiz ze cannon, while my comrades zey 'ave ze good time. I sink ze Swiss had ze most good time. But look, if zis was a real war, do you sink I would not have touched ze little lady?

MARGHERITA. What little lady?

COGNAC. Ze wife of ze master.

MARGHERITA. Lucciana?

COGNAC. Oui! C'est ça. Loucienne. I ask you. Is it right for a lovely young girl like her to be married to an old man like him when zere is a young conquering soldier in ze house?

MARGHERITA. But her husband is the richest pharmacist in town.

COGNAC. Zis monk of yours, he is sly. He dangle us all on a string. And our young king he dangle ze most of all. Before he begin, he want to swallow up ze whole world. Ha, mon dieu, if he don't remember in ze nick of time zat Lyon is still part of France, ze party was beginning already in Lyon. And now what does he do?

He talk wiz people; he take money zey give him. But mon dieu, you only give him money to keep ze most for yourself. Why don't he take it all? Huh? Me, I call everysing a spade. And I tell you zis: Ze start of my crusade, it disappoint me.

MARGHERITA. Why didn't you ransack Pisa when you were there? You could have burned all the houses down and left not a stone unturned. You could have raped all the women in Pisa to your heart's content. They're prostitutes or brothel keepers, the lot of them.

COGNAC. What pleasure is zat? I join ze war to rape decent women.

MARGHERITA. Is raping decent women more agreeable?

COGNAC. Enough of your stupid questions. Listen, tell me somesing. If I put ze wind up ze old pharmacist — you know, pretended to kill him — you sink Lucciana would srow herself at my feet? Does she love her old man?

MARGHERITA. I don't know. The stars said she had to marry him.

COGNAC. Ze stars around here, zey speak?

MARGHERITA. No. But the astrologers do. And one day in the sky, the astrologer saw that Lucciana had to marry old Manente immediately.

COGNAC. So! Tell me my beautiful old lady, does she always obey ze astrologer?

MARGHERITA. How can you fight against your destiny?

COGNAC. Alors, he want much money, zis astrologer?

MARGHERITA. He's not to be bought.

COGNAC. He do it for nosing?

MARGHERITA. Oh no. He's a great astrologer. His fees are very high just for a single consultation.

COGNAC. So he want much money. In zis house I see much money and I am not even allowed to touch it. But if I give zis money to him, I am sure his stars would speak to him in French. Holy Virgin, you are not very good to your soldiers! (*Enter Clarissa.*) Ah, God help me, here's ze ozer one now!

CLARISSA. Hello, my lovely.

COGNAC. She is worse zan you! Look.

CLARISSA. What do you two find to talk about? You're always together. Have you forgotten me?

COGNAC. Zis is no war. It's a great big nightmare.

(*Enter Lucciana.*)

LUCCIANA. Ah, here you are. I might have expected it. Well, prepare yourselves for the onslaught. Your master is in a furious temper.

(*Enter Manente.*)

MANENTE. There they are, the hussies. Two women to look after this house and my wife as well. And I don't even have a clean suit to wear.

MARGHERITA. What? Didn't you prepare the master's suit this morning, Clarissa?

CLARISSA. I thought you were doing it.

MANENTE. What did I tell you! You hear that, my dear. You hear that?

LUCCIANA. Yes, dear. I heard.

MANENTE. A fine pair. One is only good for thinking that the other, who does nothing, works.

MARGHERITA. Come now, my good master. Calm yourself. Come on, Clarissa. We'll clean your suit for you.

(*They exit.*)

COGNAC. (*to Manente*) Good morning. (*Manente looks, then turns his back.*) I say good morning because of orders. Zey tell us to be polite to ze natives so I say good morning.

MANENTE. (*to Lucciana, angrily*) You go and supervise the women.

(*Manente exits. Lucciana sits down.*)

LUCCIANA. I've given much thought to your accusations and I am convinced you were dreaming.

COGNAC. Zen I must 'ave been dreaming again last night.

LUCCIANA. It's unthinkable.

COGNAC. I swear it is true.

LUCCIANA. What? Both of them again?

COGNAC. Zey make me nervous.

LUCCIANA. Why are you still uncertain about it?

COGNAC. How can I tell in ze dark? Just when I start to sleep, one goes away and when she come back, it is not ze same one. I can't strike a light because of ze curfew, so I grope about. But alas, bos of zem feel ze same.

LUCCIANA. Why do you leave your door open?

COGNAC. Because I 'ope every night you come to see me.

LUCCIANA. Are you out of your mind?

COGNAC. If I am, you tell me and I believe it.

LUCCIANA. Ah, you Frenchmen! Always so gallant with the ladies.

COGNAC. Oh, if you listened for a while, I could tell you much more.

LUCCIANA. Are you in love with me?

COGNAC. Oui.

LUCCIANA. What happens to you when you are in love? How do you feel? What do you do?

COGNAC. I don't know. It's ze first time I get mixed up in somesing like zis.

LUCCIANA. You mean this is the first time you have ever been in love?

COGNAC. No. But it's ze first time I love a pretty young lady wiz jewels, a big house, and an old husband. You believe me?

LUCCIANA. And if I do?

COGNAC. Ah, if you only knew 'ow much I love you, you would say: I am ze most loved woman in ze whole world.

LUCCIANA. Bravo!

COGNAC. I can do even better zan zat. Would you like me to kill somebody for you? You tell me. I kill him.

LUCCIANA. My handsome little soldier offers me a corpse? Do you think I'd admire a baker who offered me bread?

COGNAC. I sink you confuse me a little.

LUCCIANA. No. I want very much to believe you love me.

COGNAC. Please believe it, Madame Lucciana. I am yours to command. I love you.

LUCCIANA. Listen. I have a little cottage in the country, with a secret room. You will go there tonight.

COGNAC. To meet you?

LUCCIANA. Yes. If you accept my conditions.

COGNAC. I accept. I accept.

LUCCIANA. Then listen carefully. You will stay there for the rest of your life and never leave that room again.

COGNAC. But why?

LUCCIANA. There'll be no reason to leave, because your loved one will always meet you there.

COGNAC. You will come, won't you?

LUCCIANA. You will see no one but me till the day you die.

COGNAC. And while I wait for you, what will I do?

LUCCIANA. Think about me.

COGNAC. Yes.

LUCCIANA. Do you live in a village in France?

COGNAC. Yes.

LUCCIANA. And you've many friends there?

COGNAC. Yes. Great friends.

LUCCIANA. You will never see them grow old. You will never know the fun they had on feast days outside the church. Or if your house has fallen into ruins or is covered with flowers. You will never know if your mother still speaks your name in her prayers. They will think you dead because you will live only for me. The army will leave without you and you'll never know if it reached Naples. Your world will cease to exist except for me alone.

COGNAC. Is it a big room?

LUCCIANA. There's a table, a chair, a bed . . . but to leave will be impossible.

COGNAC. What if some day you changed your mind and stopped coming to see me?

LUCCIANA. Must you see me in order to love me? Well now, when do you want me to shut you up in the secret room?

COGNAC. And I can never leave again?

LUCCIANA. I swear it by the Holy Virgin.

COGNAC. Bougre de bougre! You Florentine women are very strange.

LUCCIANA. And you are just a man.

COGNAC. What else do you expect me to be?

LUCCIANA. Had I loved you, I should have let myself be locked in the room.

COGNAC. You say zat because I did not ask you to do it. I am a reasonable man.

LUCCIANA. You did right, because you see, I don't love you and I should have refused.

COGNAC. Zen why all zis fuss?

LUCCIANA. I only wondered if there was such a man who could give up everything for a woman, live in obscurity, be as good as dead when she wasn't there, and see no one but her when she was with him. Tell me, my fine soldier man, how long would your great love have lasted? One week? Two weeks?

COGNAC. All ze time I stay in Florence. After zat, I should always remember you.

LUCCIANA. That's not really too bad, I suppose, for a man.

COGNAC. Now you are sad. You see, all I can do is make you sad.

LUCCIANA. Quite the contrary. I should never have forgiven you for loving me in a way he could never dream of.

COGNAC. Who? Your husband? He don't love you?

LUCCIANA. My husband? Yes, of course, my husband. Who else could I mean?

COGNAC. If he don't love you, zen why did he pay ze astrologer?

LUCCIANA. What do you say?

COGNAC. Old Margherita tell me everysing.

LUCCIANA. Margherita is a fool.

(*Enter Manente and Minutello.*)

MANENTE. (*to Cognac*) What the devil are you doing here?

COGNAC. Good morning.

MINUTELLO. Keep calm, son-in-law.

MANENTE. Keep calm? When we have savages living with us? A fine mess your damned monk's got us into with all his prophecies.

(*Enter Clarissa, Margherita, and the Peasant.*)

MINUTELLO. Brother Jerome has saved Florence from destruction.

MANENTE. So he says. I tell you, Brother Jerome brought the French here so he could chase out the Medicis.

PEASANT. That's easy enough to say now the danger has passed, thanks to Brother Jerome.

MANENTE. Look how the servants talk back at us. You can judge the situation by that.

MARGHERITA. Were things any better when you were hiding your ducats under the fountain?

MANENTE. What are you blabbering about, you old witch?

MARGHERITA. A fine mess you'd be in without him. (*to Minutello*) Eh, master?

MINUTELLO. Dame Margherita is right. Remember how scared we were? And who stepped forward to defend the country? You? Me? No. One man — Brother Jerome. Out he went on foot, all by himself to face the French army. Their king refused him audience, but Savonarola spoke to him all the same. And this time, it was the King of France who trembled and agreed to enter Florence in a garland of our flowers. And that's the truth.

MANENTE. The truth is that these barbarians . . . (*to Cognac*) Why, you vermin! (*Cognac draws his sword.*)

MINUTELLO. (*to Cognac*) Put your work tools away. And you come with me, my boy, to the council meeting. Soldier, your place is in the kitchen. Remember your king's orders.

COGNAC. Bougre de bougre!

(*The Peasant opens the door for Cognac and they both exit.*)

MINUTELLO. Come, son-in-law . . . don't worry, Lucciana. If Brother Jerome could welcome the French with flowers, he'll know how to kick them out with a few hymns.

MANENTE. That's what worries me. Brother Jerome will get all the credit and it might endanger the freedom of the state.

MINUTELLO. Do you prefer war?

MANENTE. Tyranny is also war.

MINUTELLO. I sell wool. You sell patent medicines. Let's both stay clear of politics. Come, my boy.

(*They exit. The three women begin to spin. A silence.*)

MARGHERITA. Do you think they'll start fighting with the French?

LUCCIANA. Is there any foolishness men don't commit? When they turn their minds to love, they behave like madmen. And when their minds aren't on women, they still find ways to make them miserable.

65

CLARISSA. But you aren't miserable, are you?

LUCCIANA. Me, Dame Clarissa? Why, I'm the happiest woman in the world. Didn't Margherita tell you I was Silvio's mistress? Or did she suddenly lose her tongue?

CLARISSA. Maybe she did and I forgot about it. (*pause*) So you were Silvio's mistress?

LUCCIANA. For three months. Until he fell madly in love with some gypsy dancer. Now, goodness knows who is the love of his life.

MARGHERITA. You always forbade me to talk about Silvio. Even if you asked me to.

CLARISSA. So?

LUCCIANA. I was so happy. But what was I to do? Tell my father about my condition and simply add to his worries? Or run off with some bishop to join Faustina at mass with her cardinal? Or should I have killed myself?

MARGHERITA. Hush, Lucciana, dear.

CLARISSA. Isn't Signore Manente a fine man?

LUCCIANA. Very fine. He understands the mind of an eighteen-year-old girl so perfectly.

MARGHERITA. We were really lucky finding Manente just as he was declaring his intentions. Remember how anxious we were?

LUCCIANA. I tell you, Margherita, despite my pregnancy, despite my dear father and the little importance I attach to my life, I should never have resigned myself to old Manente's bed had it not been for the horoscope. But the learned Uderigo saw my name in the stars united with Manente's. Heaven pointed the way. My destiny was stronger than my distaste. Alas! I didn't realize old men stayed young so long.

CLARISSA. And you complain. When my husband died last year . . .

LUCCIANA. Why don't we sing or something?

MARGHERITA. Sing! You don't really mean that?

LUCCIANA. Very well, then. I'll tell you about my little chat with the French soldier. He told me you both took turns going to bed with him every night.

CLARISSA. (*indignant*) Me?

MARGHERITA. (*indignant*) And you believed him?

LUCCIANA. I'd give a lot of money not to believe him.

CLARISSA. I'm a respectable woman.

LUCCIANA. I wasn't thinking about you, but about the astrologer. Margherita, tell me . . .

MARGHERITA. Cognac is a liar.

LUCCIANA. Let me finish. Tell me, what has become of Silvio in all this turmoil?

MARGHERITA. He stopped me near the Convent of San Marco yesterday. He begged me to arrange a meeting with you.

LUCCIANA. I told you before never to speak of him — either now or in the future.

MARGHERITA. But I refused to arrange the meeting.

LUCCIANA. You did well. Refusing him must have cost you a pretty penny. How many ducats did he promise in return for seeing me?

MARGHERITA. Not a penny.

LUCCIANA. Nothing! Serves me right for being so curious. Then has he finished with me forever? Why does he seek to humiliate me like this?

MARGHERITA. He wanted to see you at church so you could be first to hear the great news.

LUCCIANA. What news?

MARGHERITA. I told him then and there you were faithful to your husband.

LUCCIANA. What did he say?

MARGHERITA. He crossed himself, murmured, "May God always be with her," then he went away.

LUCCIANA. How could you let me be insulted on the streets of Florence by this good-for-nothing waster?

CLARISSA. Calm yourself, Lucciana.

MARGHERITA. Silvio . . .

LUCCIANA. Enough.

MARGHERITA. It didn't seem like he was insulting you. In fact, he was very withdrawn, almost sad.

CLARISSA. You may as well know the truth. We both thought he was getting married.

67

MARGHERITA. Forget him, Lucciana. With a little practice, you'll be surprised how easy it is to forget a man.

LUCCIANA. Do you think I've reached the stage where I can slip into bed every night with a barbarian soldier?

CLARISSA. It all started because I caught Dame Margherita coming out of his room. And she said to me, "Before you start making a fuss, go and have a talk with him." So I . . . went . . . to . . . talk . . . with him.

MARGHERITA. What about the second time?

LUCCIANA. You say he is getting married? He'll desert that woman too, one day. But at least she'll be able to remember the time Silvio wanted her forever.

MARGHERITA. You were happy once. You'll be just as happy again someday.

LUCCIANA. Was I happy with Silvio?

MARGHERITA. Do you think I'd have let him come to your room if you hadn't been happy with him?

LUCCIANA. You are right. With Silvio by my side, I was happy. Now I have lost even the memory of it. Dante overlooked that punishment in his Inferno . . . I remember and yet I don't remember. Margherita, you were with me when I was so happy. Tell me I didn't dream. I am Lucciana. Silvio kissed my body. We stayed with our lips touching hour upon hour as the night would gently fall or the dawn gently rise. And it's just as if I remembered nothing. His name — Silvio — I called out his name as he stood before me. Tell me, Margherita, did I not call out his name?

MARGHERITA. My poor child, there is still hope.

LUCCIANA. Hope? For what? Comfort from Signore Manente?

COGNAC. (*entering with the Peasant*) Have you civilian clothes to give me? I'd like to look around ze town wiz my friend here — strictly on ze quiet.

(*Enter Uderigo, Manente, Minutello.*)

MANENTE. (*to Cognac*) What the devil are you doing here?

COGNAC. Me? I wait for ze war.

UDERIGO. Well go and wait for it somewhere else.

MINUTELLO. Brother Jerome has arranged for the French to withdraw.

COGNAC. We go home?

MINUTELLO. First to Rome, then Naples.

MANENTE. Then to the devil. Away with you. Out of here.

CLARISSA. Can the peace be called off?

MANENTE. Out of here!

COGNAC. Oooh! Zat's a fine way to talk to a polite soldier. What you take me for? An obedient donkey? (*trumpets*)

UDERIGO. Trumpets. Hear them?

COGNAC. Bougre de bougre! What a crusade! (*runs off*)

CLARISSA. (*sighing*) Cognac.

MINUTELLO. You, peasant, give us something to drink. Let us toast the health of Brother Jerome.

MANENTE. Not me.

MINUTELLO. Don't let your political feelings blind you to the facts, son-in-law. Brother Jerome has freed us from this hord of savages without anyone getting hurt. He deserves our thanks.

PEASANT. Don't upset yourself, master. I'll drink to that.

MANENTE. What do you say?

PEASANT. I say that when you listen to Brother Jerome, life becomes easy. There's nothing to argue about no more; not with other people; not with yourself. Obey. It's as simple as that. Obey. It brings peace to a man.

MINUTELLO. Get back to your kitchen.

PEASANT. I'm going. Never fear. Brother Jerome cares just as much for peasants as princes. (*exits*)

UDERIGO. This sniveling little monk is becoming too important. Let's hope his power doesn't last.

LUCCIANA. What do your stars have to say?

UDERIGO. They are sad, madam.

MANENTE. They know it's bad for one party to become too strong in a country.

MINUTELLO. Why?

MANENTE. Because then man becomes too weak — and Socrates has taught me to respect the dignity of man.

69

UDERIGO. Fortunately nothing is mightier than our Holy Father. Not a day goes by without Brother Jerome hurling more abuse at Rome and the Pope.

MINUTELLO. Like all inspired orators, our good brother is sometimes given to exaggeration.

MANENTE. Exaggeration! When he calls the Holy Father Mr. Borgia!

LUCCIANA. How can you defend the Pope when he is so corrupt?

MANENTE. Hush woman! The Pope is a patron of the arts with a brilliant court. He'll silence your monk for you. Mark my words. He'll excommunicate Jerome any day now. Then maybe he'll excommunicate the merchants! Ha! Who would you sell your wool to then, eh, father-in-law?

(*Enter Giaccomo and Fra Mariano.*)

FRA MARIANO. Greetings, friends.

GIACCOMO. There's news from Rome. The Pope has spoken.

MANENTE. Socrates, Plato, and Ovid be praised. What did I tell you!

FRA MARIANO. Calm yourself, Signore Manente. Don't thank anyone yet, not even the Pope.

GIACCOMO. The Pope's offered a red hat to this Dominican, Savonarola. The red hat of a cardinal.

MANENTE. A cardinal? The Pope has made Savonarola a cardinal?

FRA MARIANO. Not quite. He wouldn't dare. He has humbly petitioned Savonarola requesting him kindly to accept the red hat, that's all.

MARGHERITA. Ah! Here's proof indeed that God inspires Brother Jerome.

GIACCOMO. I've had enough of this. Enough. It's God here, God there, God all over the place. Why can't God look after the dead in Heaven and leave us to ourselves in peace? We are old enough to know right from wrong.

MANENTE. So the Pope is buying Brother Jerome's silence, and Brother Jerome allows himself to be bought. Reasons of state — that's what they'll tell us. I ask you, my friends, if one of us behaved like present-day governments and heads of state, lying,

70

trafficking, flouting treaties, and repudiating their own signatures, would the rest of us still be friends with him? Of course not. We'd despise him because he deserved it. No businessman, however disreputable, would dare conduct himself like the governments of today.

(*Enter Bartholomeo.*)

BARTHOLOMEO. Gentlemen, I can hear you right out in the street.

MINUTELLO. What's your business here?

BARTHOLOMEO. Brother Jerome is praying for Florence to stay calm.

MANENTE. Who's side are you on?

BARTHOLOMEO. The city is awaking from its slumbers. And the friends of Brother Jerome won't let a few conspirators disrupt the destiny of our country. If you don't like our new laws, get out before we kick you out.

GIACCOMO. Bartholomeo, my dear friend, you know very well . . .

BARTHOLOMEO. I know nothing. I simply pass on orders.

MINUTELLO. How dare you come in here and show your face to me!

GIACCOMO. Where is Silvio, our old partner in crime? Why didn't you bring him along to give us some moral guidance?

BARTHOLOMEO. Silvio lives no more.

GIACCOMO. Is he dead?

BARTHOLOMEO. He's at prayer with Brother Jerome. He took the cloth of Saint Dominic this morning.

MANENTE. Jerome a cardinal, Silvio a monk, and you a moralist? Florence is not waking up. It's having nightmares.

BARTHOLOMEO. Open your eyes and see the light. If you won't see it then learn to keep your mouths shut, or your eyes won't be open much longer.

MANENTE. Father-in-law, what was that you were saying just now about freedom?

BARTHOLOMEO. Good citizens are free.

MANENTE. Then I'll become one. Tomorrow you'll see me at mass listening to Brother Jerome expounding the new virtues of the Holy Father as he accepts the cardinal's hat.

BARTHOLOMEO. Pope Borgia has offered the red hat to our beloved prior. But what will be Brother Jerome's answer?

FRA MARIANO. Do you know?

BARTHOLOMEO. Only God knows. He will dictate the answer to Brother Jerome. And tomorrow, in the church of Santa Maria del Fiore, the brother will announce it to us.

MANENTE. With all his new monks around him, no doubt. We'll go along and see the show, won't we, father-in-law? We'll take the whole family. What do you say, Lucciana? How pale you look. Good Lord, she's fainted . . .

Scene 2

The cell of Brother Jerome. The friar is alone.

JEROME. Look into the mirror, Brother Jerome.
Yes?
What do you see?
The same nose, same mouth, same eyes looking at me.
Look at your tongue.
Yes, I see it.
That tongue shapes the words which make Florence tremble with fear. Are you not amazed at such power?
No, I do not tremble at it. Why should I? Did Saint John's hand tremble when he wrote the Gospel?
Look at your cardinal's face, Brother Jerome, as you remember how your mother spanked you for peeing on the flowers.
What of it? The greatest men were small boys once, even the saints. God has willed me this power. I shall not be afraid. I shall look at myself without laughing or trembling.

My enemies expected me to be excommunicated — yet here I am, a prince of the Church. A cardinal! Me, a cardinal! How quickly things happen when one speaks with conviction. But I was wrong to accuse Pope Borgia of selling red hats for gold. I bought mine with insults. Can he be afraid of me? Corrupt, yes, I knew he was corrupt, but I never realized he was so weak. He

72

wants to silence me, but before knowing if I shall comply, he raises me up, and gives my words greater authority. Ha! The sly Roman fox overreaches himself. I see through your little game, old Pope Alexander, as clearly as God Himself. You want me to be silent, to let you die peacefully in your depravity. Then, after you're gone, I can reform the Church. But Holy Father, think of our brothers dying in sin today. How can I wait till tomorrow to save their souls? Will God wait for you to tire of your wicked ways before He judges them?

Oh, my Saviour, my life was one of peaceful contemplation until your light shook me out of my complacency. Now, I sail on a deep and stormy sea. If only I could reach the harbor . . . but I know not the way. If only I could rest, lead a tranquil life, say nothing. But it is impossible, for God's word burns in my heart. It must come out or else consume the very marrow of my bones. If this is your will, let it be done.

Today, my voice stirs the world! Not long ago, I was conducting and singing in a choir. Now, the silent people look to me from all sides, compact as metal, as a great bronze bell — and I am the hammer. I must be still or the clouds themselves will tremble and I shall have peace no more.

They expect so much of me. Always, I must be right. Because my only desire was to be surrounded by innocent children and to sing your praises, I have been hurled into a battle which leads me from monk to monk, even to the Pope himself. Here I am, a cardinal's hat within my grasp. To accept or to reject? At the carnival three years ago, even the children were drunk. But my Lord, today, the carnival will be a time for virtuous processions in honor of your mother, and young men will sing my song: "Jesus I am mad for you." Lord, I offer you Florence as a pure flower. I have separated the men from the women at night, even the husbands and wives. And I shall go on. Florence shall be chaste as you were, as I am.

Citizens, if you do not live in fear of God, the Lord will curse you for it. If you have no love for free government, I shall force such government upon you for your own good. If you refuse this

73

liberty I offer, I shall constrain you to accept it. God, I shout, "Florence, awaken from your slumbers," and Florence awakens. I look not to you older Florentines for support, for I know I must save you despite yourselves, and I have sufficient charity in my heart to compel your respect for God. Pure, untarnished youth of Florence, my appeal is to you. You are my army. Brother Jerome, take up your cross. Florence, this is the King of all the Universe. He wishes to be your king. Do you want him?

You shout, "Christ is king." I thank you. We will strain every fiber of our being in this great work.

Cardinal Jerome, look in your right hand.

Christ is in my right hand.

Look at your left hand taking the red hat. See who gives it to you and hear how the decadents laugh.

My stick will beat them into silence.

You are falling into Borgia's little trap. Alexander, with his spies, his poisons, and his gold, is more cunning than you think.

It is the Lord's will that I be strong and accept the red hat.

But not that one, Brother Jerome.

I hear you, God. I feel you close to me.

Do you think one can fight sin and still live a peaceful life?

I do not ask for peace or an end to my tribulation but for your guidance and love. Show me your power. Stretch forth your hand.

Why do you weep, Brother Jerome?

Because my God speaks to me.

My brothers, you are all assembled in this great cathedral of Santa Maria del Fiore, to hear my reply to our venerated Pope. His envoy stands among you waiting to convey my message to Rome. But my message for him is also for you. The Holy Father has offered me the red hat. Since it is the will of God, I accept it. Silence, you old decadents, and let me finish. Messenger of the Holy Father, you will tell your master I accept the red hat as he commands, but not the one he offers me. I want no hat from Borgia, no miters, big or small. I want only what God gives to his saints — death. A red hat? Yes, a hat of blood, that is what I want. Go. Take my reply to that Roman reprobate. Tell him,

I shall fight now more than ever before, and tell him further, that today Christ is king in Florence. Pray for me, my brothers.

Scene 3

Minutello's house. Manente, Minutello, Uderigo.

MINUTELLO. However furious it makes you, Savonarola is stronger than we are. Let's be realistic. Since Christ is king, Savonarola has created an eternal state.

MANENTE. Nothing is eternal except the desire for freedom in the hearts of brave men.

MINUTELLO. We are free to love Savonarola, aren't we? When a powerful man gives orders, it is only prudent to obey him.

MANENTE. Dictatorships are only passing eclipses, I tell you. I'm already an old man. Maybe I'll never see the sun again and my last days will be sad ones. But I don't despair because I suffer. The eclipse is sometimes short, sometimes long, but it is only an eclipse. Nothing more. Florence will soon be free. I know it. (*Enter Margherita and Clarissa.*)

MINUTELLO. Hush. The women are coming.

MANENTE. No one will stop me from proclaiming that spiritual and political liberty are two of man's most treasured possessions.

CLARISSA. Christ is king.

MANENTE. We know.

MARGHERITA. Christ is king.

CLARISSA. Then why don't you say it with us? (*Enter First Child.*)

FIRST CHILD. Christ is king.

MINUTELLO. Christ is king.

MARGHERITA. May the Blessed Virgin be with you.

FIRST CHILD. She is.

CLARISSA. Brother Jerome is the defender of the republic.

FIRST CHILD. Show your rosaries in the name of the Lord. (*looks at them*) Good. Yours? What's this? Silver beads? (*smashes the rosary*)

75

MARGHERITA. You little hoodlum. That rosary's been blessed!

FIRST CHILD. Your little hoodlum is one of God's creatures.

MARGHERITA. Why did you break my rosary?

FIRST CHILD. It's silver. Brother Jerome has no room for frivolities. Between our love and God's almighty power, prayers are enough. Watch it, boys. This house is suspect.

MARGHERITA. My good Lord Manente.

FIRST CHILD. Lord? Lord? Who do you dare call Lord? There's only one lord — our divine Lord in Heaven.

(*Enter three children.*)

SECOND, THIRD, AND FOURTH CHILD. Christ is king.

FIRST CHILD. Come right in! Now, all you old reprobates, in the corner with you. Over there. Come on, boys. Let's go to work.

MANENTE. What! You too, Giuseppe!

SECOND CHILD. No, uncle. I'm no longer Giuseppe. I'm one of Christ's soldiers now, and I've dug up seven copies of the *Decameron* already since this morning. Seven copies of that filthy book. I carted them over to the bonfire and washed my hands seven times.

THIRD CHILD. I've just come from there this minute. The bonfire's getting bigger and bigger. All our men are working full steam. There's books, old paintings, laces, medals, and obscene vanities from the time our Lord was not revered. It's all piling up. And tonight, Brother Jerome will burn all that garbage to the glory of God.

SECOND CHILD. Here, men! I know this house. We should get five or six volumes, at least.

FIRST CHILD. Go with him. Turn the place upside down.

MANENTE. Giuseppe!

FIRST CHILD. One move and I'll have you whipped, you stinking hypocrite.

(*Second Child and Fourth Child exit.*)

MANENTE. What are you here for?

FIRST CHILD. To teach you how to live in the name of the people, on Brother Jerome's direct orders.

UDERIGO. What do you know about life? A child of your age?

76

FIRST CHILD. Everything.

THIRD CHILD. We know God made the world in seven days, with Good and Evil. And we must love the Good.

FIRST CHILD. What's this picture?

MINUTELLO. The Holy Virgin.

FIRST CHILD. With bare arms? And rouge on her cheeks? Our Virgin Mother has no bare arms. Your painter modeled her on a common prostitute. Burn it!

MANENTE. Not my painting?

FIRST CHILD. The Holy Virgin dresses like a poor, humble woman.

MANENTE. But it's one of Botticelli's virgins.

FIRST CHILD. There's only one Virgin — she who gave birth to our Lord.

(*Second Child and Fourth Child re-enter.*)

FOURTH CHILD. These five books dishonor God.

MANENTE. Giuseppe, give me back those books . . .

SECOND CHILD. I know them. Just look at the dirty drawings.

MANENTE. They're engravings of ancient statues . . .

FIRST CHILD. You don't need these to get into Heaven. (*tears up the book*)

MANENTE. My Ovid! (*collapses*)

FIRST CHILD. We tear up paper only fit for the bonfire and you faint. You great fat pig! When you saw our souls lost in sin, did you faint then? Come, let us sing as we make Florence pure, my brothers:

> Mad for Jesus, mad for Jesus,
> Oh, what pleasure do we feel.
> We've become so mad for Jesus
> Through our love and through our zeal.
> We all shout with one accord,
> I am mad for you, my Lord.
> Mad, mad, ra, ra, ra!
> Mad, mad, ra, ra, ra!

MANENTE. (*reviving*) Mad. Yes, you are all mad.

FIRST CHILD. Mad? Us? This is rebellion. Call the chief of police.

MARGHERITA. You wouldn't have us whipped on carnival day?

FIRST CHILD. The old-time carnivals suited you best, no doubt.

77

When our older brothers got drunk and held up your skirts. Debauched old hags! How can you pray to God on silver beads
when the country is so poor?

(*Enter Silvio dressed as a Dominican monk.*)

SILVIO. Christ is king.

MINUTELLO. What! Has Brother Jerome charged the likes of you
with teaching us how to live?

SILVIO. Brother Jerome does not like impossible tasks. May it
please God to teach you only how to die.

MINUTELLO. This is my son-in-law's house. I gave it to him as
part of my daughter's dowry. I belong to the People's Party. I'm
a friend of Brother Jerome.

FIRST CHILD. This house is completely decadent. Here's a picture
of a prostitute.

MANENTE. It's one of Botticelli's. Can you still remember what that
means?

SILVIO. My friend Botticelli paints no more. He has given up such
worldly vanities. And the sculptor Michelangelo Buonarroti, who
made statues of snow for the Medicis, sculpts no more. They
are both with us now at San Marco, dedicating themselves completely to prayer. Destroy the canvas.

FIRST CHILD. Here's some books full of nude women.

MANENTE. That's the same edition of Ovid you used to read, remember? Lorenzo gave it to me . . .

FIRST CHILD. He's a real head case, he is. Tell Brother Jerome we'll
need a hammer to get through to this lot.

SILVIO. Take these vanities to the bonfire.

MANENTE. These children don't know what they're doing, but you
. . .

SILVIO. What do you mean?

MANENTE. Two years ago you'd have risked your life to save that
edition of Ovid from being destroyed . . .

SILVIO. Now my life belongs to God.

MANENTE. Surely you can't destroy such a divine work as that?

SILVIO. God alone is divine. Have him whipped for blasphemy.

MINUTELLO. Not my son-in-law!

78

FOURTH CHILD. Bet you he collapses before the fourth lash!

THIRD CHILD. Taken.

MINUTELLO. Doesn't Brother Jerome forbid betting and gambling? Let him go or I'll denounce you.

FOURTH CHILD. We bet Paters and Aves, not money.

THIRD CHILD. If he loses, he'll say twenty-five Paters. If he wins, I'll say them. And that's all right because God wins prayers either way.

FIRST CHILD. So you would denounce us, would you. Oh, if only I was a bit bigger, I'd whip you myself. But I'm not strong enough to make you howl as you should.

MANENTE. So this is what you call liberty? Eh, father-in-law? And you can support Brother Jerome.

MINUTELLO. I'll come along and do whatever I can to have you pardoned.

MANENTE. No. I want nothing from these imbeciles. Let them give me the only thing they know. I'll take the beating even if I die from it. Yet to regard death as the price for honest thought is repugnant to me. Thinking isn't an endurance test or a blood sport. It should only involve a spiritual risk.

FIRST CHILD. Tie him up. In the name of the poor starving people who have empty bellies just like mine I say, bind up tight this fat bourgeois. Whip him till he bleeds.

CLARISSA. (shouting as she exits) Mistress! Mistress! Lucciana!

SILVIO. Hand him over to the guard while I have a word with his wife. Carry on with the good work, my children.

FIRST CHILD. Christ is king.

(The children, Manente, and Minutello exit.)

SILVIO. Christ is king.

MARGHERITA. Brother Silvio, I admire you.

SILVIO. Silence, brothel keeper. I know your worth.

MARGHERITA. My worth? Why shouldn't God save me as well as the likes of you? In the days when I was worthless you were certainly no shining example yourself. But today Christ is king.

SILVIO. What are you trying to say? Come to the point.

MARGHERITA. It must be quite painful for you having to punish this

79

family. After all, once upon a time you were their friend.

SILVIO. May God give me the strength.

(*Enter Lucciana, Clarissa, and the Peasant.*)

LUCCIANA. Sir, where is my husband?

SILVIO. Being whipped, sister, at my command.

LUCCIANA. You, peasant, go and tell your friends to release him or let them whip you as well.

PEASANT. Very good, madam. (*exits*)

LUCCIANA. So you are here a second time in this house. The first time you behaved like a boor and now you are like a wild animal!

SILVIO. I carry out orders, my sister.

LUCCIANA. Will you have me whipped, too, with your orders? In bygone years, monks were never cruel, at least. You yourself would tell me they were simply narrow-minded and unclean.

SILVIO. The day I took the cloth, I washed my body to remove all the filth of the world. Since then, I think no more of my body.

LUCCIANA. Does a dirty body find more delight in the smell of angels?

SILVIO. And do you think you can seduce God with your perfumes?

LUCCIANA. Who created these perfumes, if not God?

SILVIO. God created flowers to adorn his altars and women stole his flowers from him.

LUCCIANA. Don't you read any more now that you've started burning books?

SILVIO. My prayer book is all I need.

LUCCIANA. From the time you taught me to read, you always loved good Latin. Don't the barbarisms of church Latin grate on your ears?

SILVIO. When the words declare that Almighty God will sustain me in my struggle against sin, they are clear enough. Brother Jerome wants to save your soul.

LUCCIANA. It's in no danger.

SILVIO. Our soul is always in danger. Saint Peter denied Jesus three times. Has it ever occurred to you that if he had died at that moment, he might well have died a condemned man? My confessor, Brother Jerome, who knows my life as God knows it, would like you to enter a convent.

LUCCIANA. I'm married.

SILVIO. Brother Jerome will give you dispensation.

LUCCIANA. Are you ordering me to enter a convent?

SILVIO. It's not an order.

LUCCIANA. Then you are only requesting me to do so. Why? To please you?

SILVIO. To please God.

LUCCIANA. Why should I want to please God?

SILVIO. I find it hard to believe that a woman of your spirit can be satisfied only with pleasing Manente.

LUCCIANA. You may whip Manente. You may jeer at him. But you will never make me forget my husband's most precious quality.

SILVIO. Which is?

LUCCIANA. He loves me!

SILVIO. He loves you. He loves you. Flies love milk. Bears love honey. How nice to be honey and be eaten by the bears. Your soul is pure, but it's losing direction.

LUCCIANA. Why do you still worry about my soul? Didn't you forget your past in kneeling before Brother Jerome?

SILVIO. Calm yourself! Don't let your coquettish anger get the better of you.

LUCCIANA. Yes, let us keep calm. Sit down, Silvio. (*He remains standing. She sits.*) I was just a young girl, but there was nothing adolescent about my love. I felt a love for you that could have stood the test of time and endured into old age. Let me speak, Silvio. You will have your say. Even before I became your mistress — and remember, I was once your mistress, Silvio — even before that time, I would tremble at the beauty of our love and I respected it.

SILVIO. I did wrong. I admit it. My sins horrify me. Doesn't my habit prove as much?

LUCCIANA. If you had gone to serve God the day you left me, I should have gone with you, so deep was my love. But you left me to run after a dancing girl.

SILVIO. I don't know what you are talking about.

LUCCIANA. And you know, I'm still jealous of her.

SILVIO. Lucciana, I can bring you a great happiness unthreatened by any jealousy.

LUCCIANA. Thank you. You are very kind. But please don't think I am still in love with you. I hate the name of Silvio, and I can't stand monks.

SILVIO. I shall save you as you saved me.

LUCCIANA. I saved you?

SILVIO. God moves us along strange pathways to do his bidding. Have no regrets for the Silvio you once knew. He was an evil fellow and would have made you a bad husband.

LUCCIANA. You kissed me one morning and said, "I'll see you tonight." Then off you went with a gypsy dancer to Siena and Bologna and goodness knows where else. How could you do it, Silvio? How could you?

SILVIO. Because a man without faith loves sin. When I returned home and heard you were married, I was heartbroken. The thought that I'd lost the woman of my life drove me to commit a thousand follies. I went to all the most disreputable places — and as I said then, even to church. By complete chance, I heard the prior of San Marco preaching. At the end of his sermon, I asked to become a monk. I dug graves for seven months before Brother Jerome accepted me into the brotherhood. Every evening he gave me confession, and finally, I was able to free myself from the world.

LUCCIANA. No, no, no. The lips of prostitutes once came between us. Now it's prayers. You had no soul; now you wish to be nothing else. You denied God; now you are blinded by Him. And to show me how strong your faith is, you come to my house and have my husband whipped. You order men to the stake. You are as cruel with God as you were without Him.

SILVIO. God's presence is as terrible as His absence.

LUCCIANA. Remember this dagger with its hilt shaped in the form of Venus? Add it to your bonfire of futilities.

SILVIO. I'll see to it myself. Botticelli carved it for a joke, and now

82

he is our brother. Instead of painting, he prays with me. So I shan't be sorry to throw it on the fire. But I thought this dagger was meant to protect you from men? In Manente's case, it seems to have let you down.

LUCCIANA. How dare you reproach me for Manente, you of all people. You have no right. I should have been ruined because of you had I not married. I was expecting your child. Did you know that when you ran away? Here in my stomach, my stomach which also loved you, remember? I was spared the shame of it, but not the agony of knowing that my shame could have been a great joy had you been a good man. Because if you had been my husband, our child would have lived.

SILVIO. So you married Manente without love, for fear of what people might say. Not to appear a prostitute in the eyes of the world, you prostituted yourself in the eyes of God.

LUCCIANA. What makes you think I don't love Manente?

SILVIO. Then tell me, what were your kisses worth when old Manente was later to have his share of them? You loved me, yet an excited old man could take you in his arms and believe you loved him.

LUCCIANA. Did you still love me when you came back to Florence? Had I not been married . . . but go on . . . I have only our past to comfort me in this life.

SILVIO. You are married, and I am a monk. But tell me, are you proud of your nightly lovemaking? Can you find words to express how your body wriggles in the old man's bed?

LUCCIANA. Please, Silvio!

SILVIO. Fortunately our body is but a mass of decay. I see your hands. Look at them. How white they are. How clean they seem. But I see traces of the obscene games you indulge in every night.

LUCCIANA. It's not true.

SILVIO. The hands of all women are covered with dung. I look into your eyes which have seen Manente's repulsive body. You talk of our child. He would have clutched your breasts from the moment he was born — but that was never to be. Now Manente's wrinkled mouth has taken the infant's place and I hear you gurgling like an animal in the old man's bed.

LUCCIANA. Is there no tenderness in you, Silvio?

SILVIO. Seeing me looking at your lips, and remembering the demands of Manente, don't you also wish your lips could wither into dust?

LUCCIANA. Don't torture me anymore.

SILVIO. When one has a memory, is there anything on earth more repugnant than a woman's lips? Do you expect me to be mortified with grief because I can no longer have what someone else possesses? Do not weep. Have no regrets. What were those grotesque nights worth? Awaiting God and a Christian death is the most beautiful night of love.

LUCCIANA. Why did you not love me as you love God, Silvio?

SILVIO. I do love you, my sister.

LUCCIANA. Yes. Like a good monk. Why didn't you love me when you had the chance?

SILVIO. Listen to me. I wish to please God. I fear Hell not because of its torments but simply because in Hell, God is not visible. And I want to see God. Yet if my eternal damnation could give you entry to Paradise, Lucciana, I should damn myself that you might be saved and might still think of me when you were alone before God.

LUCCIANA. Silvio!

SILVIO. Call me "Brother" — and enter a convent.

LUCCIANA. No. It's not God I love, but you. I swear to you, Silvio, I shall pray every night that God may bring us together again in Heaven. And I also swear that from this day, I shall live in my house like a widow.

SILVIO. Let us kneel down and pray, my sister.

CURTAIN

84

ACT III

Scene 1

Two years later. The living room of what is now Manente's house. Manente, Fra Mariano (now slightly gray), Giaccomo, Uderigo, and a butcher are in discussion. The atmosphere is one of gloom, dispiritedness, dismay.

BUTCHER. What about me? Do you think my life's a bed of roses? It's no joke living in Florence these days, let me tell you. It's enough to make you sick. And on top of everything . . . oh, what's the use of complaining all the time?

UDERIGO. Complaining makes one feel better. But now he won't even let us do that. He's even poisoned our friendships. If one of us here were a spy, the rest of us would be in prison by tonight.

BUTCHER. He needs no spy to find out what I think. I'm a butcher and he orders everybody to stop eating meat out of love for Christ the king and because the city hasn't enough money to buy animals anyway. How can he expect my union to support his government when it orders no meat six days out of seven? I mean to say! I'm a butcher.

MANENTE. I haven't had a good night's rest in six years. And why? Because for six years, I've been so eager to wake up every morning and hear the first workman shout to me as he passes my house, "Hey friend, have you heard the good news? Savonarola is dead."

OTHERS. Sssshh! Hush! Not so loud!

MANENTE. For six long years, I've waited for the sun to rise on that day.

(There is a pause.)

UDERIGO. Your sister-in-law certainly believes in taking her time, my good Manente.

GIACCOMO. Faustina always kept people waiting even before she became a great lady of Rome.

85

FRA MARIANO. Can't she understand there is a limit to our patience?

MANENTE. Margherita! Hey there! Margherita! You old witch!

MARGHERITA. (*appearing*) Christ is king.

GIACCOMO. (*aside*) And you're a cow!

MARGHERITA. You called me, my sweet master?

MANENTE. What's keeping my sister-in-law?

MARGHERITA. Such an attractive lady needs a rest after traveling three days from Rome.

FRA MARIANO. But she's been resting four hours now.

MANENTE. Go and tell her to hurry up, you old windbag.

MARGHERITA. My sweet master, sleeping is the only work that can't be hurried. Can you sleep quickly?

MANENTE. Go back to her.

MARGHERITA. Christ is king. (*exits*)

MANENTE. Poor Christ! How he must regret the vagueness of his teaching as he looks down at us with Plato and Homer from his Kingdom of Shadows. I only hope the next time a man becomes famous after he's dead, God has made his words of marble that can't be deformed. Unfortunately, our dear friend from Galilee had that subtle, paradoxical Jewish turn of mind — which always leads to catastrophe.

(*Enter Faustina.*)

GIACCOMO. Faustina.

FRA MARIANO. Dear sister Faustina.

MANENTE. Faustina. And not before time.

FAUSTINA. Please, friends. Calm yourselves.

MANENTE. I told you when you arrived, Faustina, not to make fun of us. You live in Rome, governed by a liberal Pope, a patron of the arts, while we Florentines are just miserable wretches.

UDERIGO. Savonarola even forbids me to read the stars. Yet they were there even before Jesus. And didn't the three Wise Men follow one of them?

GIACCOMO. What a miserable life!

UDERIGO. He made me bow my head; and my eyes which interpreted the sky were cast down onto the points of my shoes.

FRA MARIANO. This swine must be exterminated.

MANENTE. Easier said than done. Savonarola is chaste. The kind of life he imposes on us he leads by choice. He's an ascetic, a celibate, an enemy of the arts . . .

BUTCHER. And a vegetarian.

FRA MARIANO. Well, I say this celibate swine must be exterminated.

FAUSTINA. Oh, how you complain! In the old days, Florence used to sing. Has Brother Jerome's preaching driven you to such a state that you shout and scream like wild men?

GIACCOMO. Rome has excommunicated Savonarola, and he just laughs.

FRA MARIANO. Laughing at excommunication! I don't know why the Pope tolerates it.

UDERIGO. Savonarola even dares to say Mr. Borgia is corruption personified.

FAUSTINA. You speak to me as if I were the Pope. In Rome, I'm only a cardinal's mistress.

MANENTE. Don't talk like that, Faustina. Rome's reputation is bad enough as it is.

FAUSTINA. Is Florence completely out of its mind?

MANENTE. No, but we live in fear of the whip.

FAUSTINA. My poor friends.

UDERIGO. It's nothing to joke about. If you'd been whipped for an hour, you'd shudder at the very thought of it.

GIACCOMO. The brutes!

MANENTE. And you don't know the half of it. Have you seen Lucciana? She's just like all the other women in Florence. They're mad, the lot of them. Now Lucciana isn't even my wife any more.

GIACCOMO. They don't have lovers, either. They are all abstainers, by government order, even with their own husbands.

FAUSTINA. Dear brother-in-law, I can't tell you how sorry I am. She's such a pretty girl to be serving no purpose. Has it been long?

BUTCHER. Oh, they bleed us like sheep.

FAUSTINA. Do you have the same problem?

BUTCHER. Me? No, my wife's dead. But I'm a butcher.

FRA MARIANO. He's a prophet of the devil.

FAUSTINA. Why do you think he's a prophet?

GIACCOMO. We don't.

MANENTE. But everybody else does.

FAUSTINA. Why?

UDERIGO. Because he makes prophecies.

FRA MARIANO. He claims God talks to him.

GIACCOMO. As if prophets could exist these days.

FAUSTINA. I simply must take a dozen Florentine couples back to Rome with me. The Pope grows so tired of his clever little monkeys. I know he'll just adore you. Don't you see? You are like a species of some strange monster we thought extinct.

GIACCOMO. You may mock at us, Faustina, but I'd give my life to liberate Florence.

BUTCHER. Me too.

FAUSTINA. Would you, Fra Mariano?

FRA MARIANO. Me? Why certainly. Anything to shut up this false prophet. Because God doesn't speak to him. After all, does God speak to me?

FAUSTINA. Perhaps God does speak to you. Only you don't know how to listen to Him.

MANENTE. Stop your teasing, Faustina.

FAUSTINA. I've never been more serious in my whole life. Now I think about it, I've always been a serious person.

GIACCOMO. You?

FAUSTINA. Isn't a serious person one who never misses a chance to laugh?

UDERIGO. If you'd lived in Florence these last few years . . .

FAUSTINA. God's been speaking to me for years. Why are you all deaf? Why let Brother Jerome have the monopoly of celestial voices? Good Fra Mariano, when you preached in the old days before Brother Jerome changed the popular taste, didn't you speak as eloquently as he did?

FRA MARIANO. I preached better.

FAUSTINA. Wouldn't you be a prophet if you made prophecies too?

FRA MARIANO. She's right. Why shouldn't I talk like he does and say God speaks to me too?

88

MANENTE. Even if God really spoke to Fra Mariano and to nobody else, the people of Florence would still believe in Savonarola. When our good friend here revealed his divine words, they'd just laugh at him.

FRA MARIANO. (*annoyed*) Why should they?

FAUSTINA. Brother-in-law, you're an old donkey.

UDERIGO. You seem to regard us as a source of amusement, Faustina. But you won't laugh long because we want no part in your little game. If you're really serious in what you say, you're insane and should be put away. For such mad notions will only bring more painful worries on our heads.

FAUSTINA. A foolish remark said calmly before three intelligent people remains a foolish remark. But add another ten thousand people, shout your foolish remark to them with a certain *savoir-faire* and you'll be acclaimed. For there is nothing more stupid than a gathering of ten thousand intelligent people. Fra Mariano, make your prophecies in front of ten thousand people and you will be a prophet.

FRA MARIANO. Now that's what I call sensible thinking.

FAUSTINA. God spoke to me last night about you.

FRA MARIANO. (*flushing with pleasure*) God spoke to you about me?

MANENTE. (*reproachfully*) Faustina!

FAUSTINA. And do you know what he said? God told you . . .

FRA MARIANO. God told me . . .

FAUSTINA. . . . that Brother Jerome is a false prophet.

FRA MARIANO. (*triumphant*) Just what I said. Brother Jerome is a false prophet. Quite right.

FAUSTINA. And you will prove it.

FRA MARIANO. And I will prove it.

FAUSTINA. By climbing alive onto a flaming pyre.

FRA MARIANO. By climbing alive onto a flaming . . . What! You're mad.

FAUSTINA. (*continuing*) You are the true prophet . . .

FRA MARIANO. I'll make my prophecies on my own.

FAUSTINA. . . . and Brother Jerome is an imposter. God wants you to prove the truth of your words by commanding Brother Jerome to accompany you onto the flaming pyre. God will burn Brother Jerome to punish him for his falseness whilst you, the chosen one of God, will remain untouched and smiling in the center of the flames.

FRA MARIANO. God told me nothing like that, my friends. She's raving.

FAUSTINA. Savonarola must prove the truth of his prophecies and submit to this Heavenly judgment.

FRA MARIANO. Would you put your backside on red-hot coals if you didn't want to get burnt? Fire burns. Everybody knows that, and God better than anyone else.

FAUSTINA. You must challenge Savonarola. I think we'd all be very interested to hear his reply.

FRA MARIANO. What if he accepts! This whole business is . . . is . . . like some fairy tale. (*to Butcher*) Would you jump into the Arno if you didn't want to get wet?

FAUSTINA. Will you climb onto the pyre with Savonarola or not? For six years he has been speaking to Florence in the name of God. Now we are asking him to submit to God's judgment. Wouldn't you like to hear him refuse?

UDERIGO. You are clever, Faustina, but Brother Jerome is even cleverer than the most skillful woman.

FRA MARIANO. Clever! Clever! Oh yes. Very clever, climbing onto a bonfire to avoid getting burned.

FAUSTINA. Weren't you ready to give your life to liberate Florence?

FRA MARIANO. I still am — on condition I die like everybody else, from natural causes.

FAUSTINA. Will common sense never produce heroes?

FRA MARIANO. Heroes? Heroes are fine as long as they are somebody else. But just imagine being one yourself. Visualize every detail. Whew! I'm sweating like a bull. That cursed fire is burning me already.

(*He drinks. For some time a child has been observing the proceedings through the window.*)

FIRST CHILD. (*whistles*) Hey, fellows. Here, quickly. (*shouting into room*) Nobody move!

MANENTE. Heaven help us. Now you'll find out what Florence is really like, Faustina.

(*Enter three children.*)

SECOND CHILD. Nobody move.

FIRST CHILD. (*at window*) I'll be right there.

(*He whistles again. Margherita and Clarissa enter.*)

MARGHERITA. The police are outside in the street. (*sees the children*) Oooh! Christ is king. Christ is king!

CLARISSA. Holy mother of God preserve us.

THIRD CHILD. Silence, you smelly old bags!

FIRST CHILD. (*entering*) So, you plot here. Are you the prophet? (*sniffs at the wine flagon*) An alcoholic prophet!

BUTCHER. Oh God, what is to become of us?

SECOND CHILD. What are you moaning about?

BUTCHER. I'll be whipped, on top of everything else. What's a butcher doing on earth at a time like this!

FOURTH CHILD. (*to Fra Mariano*) This time, you'll get a double dose, you can count on it.

FRA MARIANO. Oh no. No more whippings, please.

SECOND CHILD. Why not? You drunken sot!

FRA MARIANO. It hurts.

(*The children howl with laughter.*)

UDERIGO. What are you trying to accuse us of?

FIRST CHILD. I've been hiding under your windows for a whole week. And I've heard enough to march the lot of you to the gallows.

CLARISSA. Oh!

MANENTE. Perhaps you didn't understand what we said.

FIRST CHILD. I didn't understand any of it, that's just the point. When a man speaks like a Christian, other Christians can understand him.

BUTCHER. Why you little brats! I'll flatten the lot of you. I'll hang you up by your toenails.

FIRST CHILD. One more step and I'll recommend you for special treatment. (*to Fra Mariano, with exaggerated sweetness*) Well now, so you are the so-called prophet, eh? Explain yourself more clearly, good Fra Mariano.

UDERIGO. (*playing all-out*) You are quite right. God has spoken to our brother here.

SECOND CHILD. Let us sit down, comrades.

FIRST CHILD. Okay. Let's have it.

FAUSTINA. You boys, listen to me, and the women too. This brother has been given a message for Florence.

FRA MARIANO. No. No. No.

FAUSTINA. You are simply an instrument in the hands of Providence, and you must fulfill your duty to the end. The Lord has visited Fra Mariano and made various revelations to him.

FRA MARIANO. I'm not revealing anything.

FIRST CHILD. Do you want the whip right now?

FRA MARIANO. Oh no!

FIRST CHILD. Then shut up.

FAUSTINA. Take him straight to your leaders. He will tell them just what he told us — that God orders him to climb onto a big flaming pyre.

FRA MARIANO. Oh! Oh!

CHILDREN. No kidding! Really? Bravo! We'll give him a hand. Bags me to light the fire!

FRA MARIANO. Oh!

FAUSTINA. The Lord told him . . . oh, I hardly dare repeat it . . . well anyway, they're either the words of the Lord for which I am not responsible or else Fra Mariano is an imposter and you can sort that out with him.

FIRST CHILD. Don't you worry.

FRA MARIANO. I haven't said a word.

FAUSTINA. The Lord wants to silence His enemies once and for all. He has asked the Franciscan and Dominican champions, Fra Mariano and Brother Jerome, to climb onto a pyre together. The imposter will be burnt alive, says the Lord, while the other monk, encircled by flames, will sing to the glory of Florence and come out unharmed.

MARGHERITA. A miracle?

92

FAUSTINA. A miracle!

CLARISSA. Oh, my poor Mariano. You'll be burned alive. The Lord is bound to save Brother Jerome.

CHILDREN. Great! That's fine! Boy oh boy! What a blaze. Come on, prophet, come and be roasted like a chicken.

FIRST CHILD. Let us pray first for our good Brother Jerome who will come from the fire singing our hymns.

FRA MARIANO. Uderigo, save me.

FOURTH CHILD. He's got the wind up already.

FRA MARIANO. These children are mad. Faustina's mad. Everybody's mad.

SECOND CHILD. God wants you to climb onto the pyre with Brother Jerome. And you'll do just that.

THIRD CHILD. Let's go, comrades. We'll announce the miracle in every street.

MARGHERITA. (*calling Lucciana*) My lady, my lady! Come quickly. Brother Jerome's going to do a miracle.

CLARISSA. Lucciana will be so happy.

(*The two old ladies go off to Lucciana's rooms.*)

MANENTE. (*to Faustina*) What if Brother Jerome were not burnt? Don't you even believe in witchcraft? (*Faustina laughs.*)

FIRST CHILD. (*shouting toward the street*) Brother Jerome will confound the sinful!

SECOND CHILD. Have you seen a miracle before?

THIRD CHILD. No.

CHILDREN. Long live Brother Jerome!

GIACCOMO. Long live Fra Mariano!

FRA MARIANO. Oh!

SECOND CHILD. He'll be the one to get fried.

GIACCOMO. What do you know about it?

SECOND CHILD. Who, me?

FAUSTINA. God will choose, my children.

FIRST CHILD. God's chosen already. Come on. Let's get going.

FAUSTINA. Keep a close guard on Fra Mariano, my friends, and go along with the children.

FRA MARIANO. But I don't want to go! No. No.

CHILDREN. Long live the miracle. Quick march.

(*Margherita and Clarissa return, followed by Lucciana.*)

MARGHERITA. Come along, Clarissa. Let's go and tell our friends about Brother Jerome's bonfire. Hurry up!

CLARISSA. He's going to sing for us in the flames. Christ is king.

MARGHERITA. Christ is king! You can say that again. Come on. You lead the way.

(*They exit leaving only Faustina and Lucciana onstage. The children sing hymns in the streets.*)

LUCCIANA. Have you no shame?

FAUSTINA. Why?

LUCCIANA. Aren't you sorry for what you said to me just now?

FAUSTINA. I don't follow you, really.

LUCCIANA. Why don't you take hold of yourself and try to save your soul even at this late hour?

FAUSTINA. What late hour? Oh, I see, you're upset about the monks challenging each other in combat.

LUCCIANA. This is no combat.

FAUSTINA. Then what do you call this entertainment?

LUCCIANA. Aren't you even afraid of Hell?

FAUSTINA. All in good time. Today, it's the miracle pyre. Tomorrow, a pearl necklace. After that . . .

LUCCIANA. What pearl necklace?

FAUSTINA. The one Pope Borgia will give me, of course, when I tell him about my new method of arbitration. He'll want to put it into general practice. He finds useless discussions so tiresome. Don't you? So, to the fire with them and let the survivor come and see me. He'll have won his case. It's a perfectly wonderful way to arbitrate!

LUCCIANA. So this is how you laugh at us.

FAUSTINA. My dear little sister, do you honestly believe one of those monks will come out of the fire alive?

LUCCIANA. God created the world in seven days. Why shouldn't he part the flames for our brother? They're much lighter to move than the waters of the Red Sea!

FAUSTINA. Are you always like this, even on days without mira-

94

cles? You haven't changed a bit. Or should I say, you've turned out as expected, an old stick in the mud.

LUCCIANA. I despise you.

FAUSTINA. You are not very charitable for all your Christianity. And on miracle days, sins must count double.

LUCCIANA. Why did you have to come back to Florence?

FAUSTINA. Come now, Lucciana. Don't be so aggressive. We're sisters, remember, and I love you.

LUCCIANA. Did you love us when you left poor father in shame with only me to comfort him?

FAUSTINA. You didn't have much idea how to manage your life either. How could you marry Manente and expect to remain faithful to him when you still love Silvio?

LUCCIANA. Do you think you ran away yesterday? Florence has changed in the last six years, and so have our hearts. Yes, I love Brother Silvio, but my love is quite different from yours.

FAUSTINA. Do you mean you don't love Silvio as a woman loves a man? That you are not sorry he's a monk? Or that — to use your own little cliché — he has found his salvation? You are not sorry he is wasting his life just as you are wasting yours? Is that what you mean?

(*Enter Brother Silvio.*)

LUCCIANA. Silvio. Help me. I'm being pursued by a devil.

SILVIO. Faustina!

FAUSTINA. Well, well! Silvio . . .

SILVIO. Brother Silvio. Have you heard the wonderful news? Brother Jerome is going before God to save the last stray sheep of Florence.

FAUSTINA. Has he accepted Fra Mariano's challenge?

SILVIO. When he heard it, he fell silent. Then he slowly withdrew to his cell where he is now at prayer.

FAUSTINA. Oh, I wish tomorrow were here.

LUCCIANA. Yes. For your salvation.

FAUSTINA. Don't make me say things I shouldn't before the proper time. All I'll say is that tomorrow we'll be out of here, all three of us, and on our way. I'll have saved you and you'll both finally be happy in each other's arms.

SILVIO. What's this, you Roman slut?

FAUSTINA. I say this woman loves you as you love her, and you are both acting like children.

LUCCIANA. Make her be quiet, Fra Silvio.

FAUSTINA. Like two unhappy children wasting your lives living a lie.

LUCCIANA. Please, Fra Silvio, make her stop.

FAUSTINA. Haven't you longed night after night to take her in your arms? And as you clasped your hands a thousand times in prayer, haven't you thought only of clasping her hands? Admit it!

LUCCIANA. May God forgive her.

FAUSTINA. Why the hurry to speak when you have nothing to say? Are you afraid of his answer? Which one? That he'll confess his love or that he'll try to persuade you there's nothing there any more?

LUCCIANA. Don't answer, Brother Silvio.

SILVIO. And if all these things you say are true?

LUCCIANA. When he came back, I was married, alas!

FAUSTINA. What of it! You won't be the first to commit adultery. What other sin is there for a woman except to fall and disfigure herself? (*to Silvio*) Look at me, and tell me how many men I have loved. Adultery leaves no traces.

SILVIO. She is right. Brother Jerome insists that we live with either God or the devil on this earth. There is no other choice. God or the devil. And she is the devil.

LUCCIANA. Yes. You are the devil.

FAUSTINA. Little parrot!

LUCCIANA. Do you have to insult me?

FAUSTINA. Parrot? It's no insult. It's a wonderful animal. A talking bird. I'd never seen or heard of them before, until some sailors of Isabella the Catholic brought them back from their travels to the New Indies. Haven't you heard about it in Florence? Well, someone discovered the world was round, just like an orange.

SILVIO. So they have returned from their great voyage?

FAUSTINA. Yes. With red-skinned men and talking birds and some gold — though not very much. At least the queen sent her apologies to the Pope.

LUCCIANA. Do you think it's true about the talking birds, Silvio?

FAUSTINA. Non-human mouths speaking words. But don't let them upset your prayers. You know, these birds fly in the clouds and see the earth from above. They are covered with feathers and use their beak to talk with.

LUCCIANA. (*to Silvio*) She is joking, isn't she? (*to Faustina*) What do they say, these birds of yours?

FAUSTINA. Nothing about Heaven. Nothing about unknown worlds. They don't even tell us the secrets of the animals, but simply repeat the words men teach them. Nothing more, my little parrot.

LUCCIANA. (*to Silvio*) Ah, so much the better. Now perhaps you won't feel so sorry about missing that voyage. You wanted to go with those sailors, didn't you, Silvio?

FAUSTINA. Silvio?

LUCCIANA. Yes.

FAUSTINA. Weren't you afraid to believe the world was round?

LUCCIANA. I stopped him going.

FAUSTINA. Why?

LUCCIANA. So that he could love me and I could be his wife.

SILVIO. I discovered a much greater world, Lucciana, thanks to you, because you made me discover Heaven. Our life together on earth was no longer possible, Lucciana, yet I couldn't bear to lose you. I had to believe in immortality so that you could be immortal. I can tell you now, for tomorrow, when Brother Jerome goes up into the flames, God will speak to us. I suffered. (*to Faustina*) Yes, you are right, you fallen woman. (*to Lucciana*) Neither this habit I wear nor your love spared me the most terrible torments. Night after sleepless night, I lived with but one image: your honeymoon night with Manente. I could hear you. I could see him. I watched you both. Everything that the imagination of a lonely man can make our body endure, I endured. (*to Faustina*) But what of it? What does it all prove?

FAUSTINA. That you are miserable and I'm happy. Yes, happy.

SILVIO. For how long?

FAUSTINA. You don't frighten me with all your talk of Savonarola staring at death. Huh, what a way to be happy, always living with death.

SILVIO. Remember that your body is already destined to be a corpse, that our houses are already graveyards and that in thirty years we will all be dead.

FAUSTINA. All the more reason for finding happiness right now at any price.

SILVIO. You think you are happy? No, of course not. Because you despise your joy. You despise your laughter. You resign yourself to it, that's all. You say: "Life holds nothing better, so I'll take what I can get." Whereas I despise all that is despicable in me. And so when I am happy, at least I can love my happiness.

FAUSTINA. I can understand man's desire to create God in order to find comfort and an explanation for everything from the stars to his own emotions. But what I do not understand is that one day, in the great void, God had the desire to create man.

LUCCIANA. Answer her, Silvio.

SILVIO. Don't despair, Lucciana. We shall be together in Paradise.

FAUSTINA. And what will you do with Manente in Paradise? Ha, much good that will do you denying each other on earth in the hope of coming together again in Paradise. You won't be such fools tomorrow, thank God. And while you are waiting for your Paradise, I'll take you both to Rome. I'll arrange for Pope Borgia to release Silvio from his vows. He understands all about life and women. Then you can both lie low in my house until Manente dies.

SILVIO. Pay no heed to this devil's disciple, Lucciana. We shall be saved. God will speak to Brother Jerome.

FAUSTINA. My poor Silvio. God speaks to him just like the birds of the Indies. He simply re-echoes what Brother Jerome says. God is the biggest parrot of them all.

LUCCIANA. Might Silvio have sacrificed both our lives for a parrot?

SILVIO. Before one o'clock, Brother Jerome will be singing our hymns in the fire, and Faustina will be praying on her knees with us. (*Enter Bartholomeo.*) Christ is king, Bartholomeo.

BARTHOLOMEO. Brother Jerome has left his cell. He wants to see you.

SILVIO. I shall go and kneel with our brothers at the pyre.

FAUSTINA. What time is the miracle?

BARTHOLOMEO. There won't be any miracle. Brother Jerome has refused the challenge.

SILVIO. What?

LUCCIANA. He's refused to prove God speaks to him?

BARTHOLOMEO. He says man is at the service of God, not God at the service of man.

FAUSTINA. Oh, he's a clever one, this Brother Jerome. Why didn't he come to Rome! My house would have been at his disposal. Once a cardinal, there was nothing to prevent him from becoming Pope. The Holy Father wasn't against having him as his successor. In fact, he favored having a strict Pope now and again to serve as a good example.

(*Re-enter Fra Mariano and his party of friends.*)

GIACCOMO. Come in, come in, good Brother Mariano.

FRA MARIANO. I'm coming, my friends. I'm coming. I'll sit down, Manente, if I may. And I'll have a little of your excellent wine. Isn't this Brother Silvio I see?

FAUSTINA. You are very gay for a prophet.

UDERIGO. I suppose you already know the news, Faustina, since I see Bartholomeo is here.

BARTHOLOMEO. (*to Silvio*) See you tonight, Brother. Christ is king! (*He exits. The others sneer.*)

FRA MARIANO. I'm parched, Manente.

MANENTE. Lucciana, I didn't notice you welcoming my friends. (*Lucciana makes a greeting and exits. The four children enter.*)

FIRST CHILD. (*pointing to Fra Mariano*) Here he is, the vulgar loudmouth.

MANENTE. All right. That's enough out of you. From now on, if you want to shout, go and shout at your leaders. Tell them they might at least have the courage to prove their prophecies.

99

(*Enter Margherita and Clarissa, out of breath.*)

MARGHERITA. (*to Silvio*) Isn't there going to be anything? Not even a teeny-weeny little bit of a miracle?

CLARISSA. What a shame!

BUTCHER. (*to Margherita*) I'll bring a leg of mutton tonight. Maybe two legs. And you can cook them for us. We might as well use that bonfire for something.

FRA MARIANO. I told Savonarola he was a liar. Yes indeed. I challenged him to climb onto the pyre with me so that God could choose between us. Ha! And he was afraid of God's judgment.

GIACCOMO. And as he became more frightened, you became more courageous.

FIRST CHILD. Brother Jerome was not afraid. He simply felt it was improper for him, as our leader, to accept the challenge of a small-fry monk like you.

SILVIO. And I say you are the liar, Fra Mariano. For God never spoke to a debauched old drunkard like you. Brother Jerome is a prophet, I tell you. I'll climb onto the flaming pyre with you myself so that God may make his choice and confound you.

LUCCIANA. Oh no!

FAUSTINA. I forbid you, Silvio. Let me explain . . .

SILVIO. Go and announce everywhere that I challenge this man, and that he'll be lashed to death if he refuses to go with me into the fire.

CHILDREN. Christ is king! Christ is king!

Scene 2

Brother Jerome is in his cell.

JEROME. Brother Jerome, go to the people and have the courage to tell them what you think: that your friends have lost their senses; that proof by fire is sheer folly; that man has no right to provoke God. All is lost, Savonarola. Their desire for a miracle is greater than your power. What should I do? Go to the pyre, nevertheless? Help our disobedient Brother Silvio? And do all I can to prevent

100

this proof by fire? Yet if he should climb into the flames? Lord, perhaps I have not sufficient confidence in your love? You know I tried to prevent this miracle for which they clamor — but to no avail. Grant me this miracle, Lord. You can't forsake me now. You will save me, Lord, I know that. But how? How?
(*Trumpets, bells, singing.*)

Scene 3

The town square. The principal characters march quickly past, each indicating his feelings. The Butcher embraces Uderigo who, in turn, indicates the sky to Manente, etc. The procession ends with the children.

THIRD CHILD. (*to Second Child*) Here, take these pointed sticks.

FOURTH CHILD. What are they for?

SECOND CHILD. Are they very sharp? (*pricks the First Child who shouts out*)

THIRD CHILD. Try this one as well.

FIRST CHILD. No. No.

SECOND CHILD. When they've arrested Savonarola, they'll be taking him through the streets to the prison. So we'll try and jab him in the backside with these sticks.

FIRST CHILD. Why us? We sang his psalms. We were his army.

SECOND CHILD. Not any more. He backed out of his miracle.

FIRST CHILD. He didn't back out of anything.

THIRD CHILD. (*threateningly*) Did you see any miracle?

FIRST CHILD. God made it rain to put out the fire.

FOURTH CHILD. A thunder shower is no miracle.

SECOND CHILD. Did you see Silvio surrounded by flames, yes or no?

THIRD CHILD. Did you hear him singing psalms on a flaming pyre?

FIRST CHILD. But the Franciscan refused to climb up with Fra Silvio.

SECOND CHILD. Then why didn't Silvio climb up on his own?

FOURTH CHILD. Because of Savonarola. I saw him.

FIRST CHILD. Silvio was going to climb up alone anyway to sing our psalms. Then God put the fire out.

101

FOURTH CHILD. Water putting out a fire, that's no miracle.

THIRD CHILD. He was scared as a rabbit of the fire.

FIRST CHILD. That's not true. Fra Silvio wasn't scared at all.

SECOND CHILD. He should have climbed on the pyre, then.

FOURTH CHILD. Savonarola held him back by his habit. I saw him.

FIRST CHILD. Why?

THIRD CHILD. Because Savonarola is a false prophet.

SECOND CHILD. Yes, a false prophet.

(*Noise of bells, fireworks, shouts, etc.*)

FOURTH CHILD. Listen.

THIRD CHILD. The Convent of San Marco, it's on fire. (*bells*)

SECOND CHILD. They've got Savonarola.

THIRD CHILD. Let's go prick his arse for him.

SECOND CHILD. (*to First Child*) You not coming?

(*They prick his bottom. First Child shouts and cries.*)

FOURTH CHILD. (*calling Second Child and Third Child*) Come on, quick. I don't want to miss this. (*The three children exit.*)

FIRST CHILD. (*alone, on his knees*) Christ is king. Christ is king. (*He sobs. Noises of battle, music, then a long silence.*)

Scene 4

A cell which looks like that of a monk. Brother Jerome is alone.

JEROME. They have attacked my convent, killed my disciples, broken my limbs. They have judged me and I shall be hanged. The serene judges, with untroubled conscience, bound me hand and foot and cast me into a dark dungeon, far from my friends. There, by candlelight, in the absence of God, they silently tortured me on the rack to the point of death. Jerome! Oh, poor Jerome! As you cried out in agony from the depths of that dungeon, they listened to you as a hunter listens to a trapped animal. How can those who are happy ever understand the horror of a man utterly alone whose muscles are being torn from him one by one! Oh Christ, you suffered on the cross a whole twilight. Now I know how interminable such times can be. But my agony has lasted twenty-seven days. Twenty-seven times the sun has risen on a new day of torture, and sometimes they wake me at night.

That first Sunday when the guards led me across the city to change prisons, the little children who had sung my psalms came and pierced my body with their pointed sticks. My enemies are triumphant. My friends have forsaken me. God is silent. Brother Jerome, you are undone. (*weeps*) Jesus, when I prayed for a martyr's death, I was praying for your crown of thorns, your crown of blood in a great expanse of deserted countryside. But you press me into a dungeon without a word. To what purpose were my cries, my suffering? I am unsoiled by woman. I am a stranger to joy. Why, then, have you forsaken me? The cowardice of man I can understand. But your silence terrifies me. Am I no longer your Brother Jerome? Jesus who loved me, see my wounds, see my despair. Jesus . . . I am alone . . . you have deserted me in this last hour. Jesus.

Our enemies prepared a trap for us. I scented it, but alas, Silvio accepted the challenge against my will. You are brave, Silvio. You, also, have been tortured for twenty-seven days and have not cried out. They applied the shackles and waited for your screams — but all they heard was the sound of your breaking bones. Why did you require this miracle, Silvio? Why did you need proof of my teaching by casting yourself into the flames? Was your faith so unsure? Or was it only to convince the unbelievers, and one woman in particular? Now my work will perish because you had to save one solitary woman. Yours is not a saintly nature, Silvio. A saint does not choose between sinners, but takes all the sins of all sinners upon himself and remains silent. You wanted to throw yourself in the face of death. You had the soul of a hero, that is all. But how can I think of my friends' faults and forget my own? What sins have I committed? Answer me, God, here is a chance to speak. I have committed no sin. You came to me because Italy was so corrupt. I fought against that corruption. The rich were too rich, the poor too poor. Petty princes were all rending Italy apart and I wished to unify it. I attacked sin. Was I too impatient? Was I too hard? But Lord, was the gate of Hell not open, and your punishment so terrible? How could I wait to save those who were losing their way?

You have all told me that for six years I prevented men and women from being happy in the name of Christ. This is untrue. I led them back to virtue. Is virtue so sad a prospect for corrupted souls? Then let them be cured. I have reminded you many times that there are but two guides in this world, God and the devil. We all must make our choice: debauchery or the convent. You say I lacked a sense of charity? But charity is a dangerous thing, for it benumbs the one you wish to save. When I gave food to the poor, it was not to fill their bellies, but rather that they might find their salvation. What would be the point of filling a belly which is already decayed? Lord, before speaking in your name, I looked at the lives of men. I saw they had lost their paradise and were not happy.

Then where is my error, Lord? Tell me! Silvio was an evil ruffian. I turned him from sin. His legs are broken. Tomorrow they will take him to be hanged. But his soul is pure and you will receive him into your Holy Paradise. Lord, how silent you are. Will you not look upon me, at least, and see my undoing?

I speak to provoke your answer, for I am sure of nothing any more and I tremble. Since I was a child, my only thought has been to offer you my soul. You wished me to go amongst my brothers and sisters and guide them towards eternal happiness. I tried. But that too is an impossible task. Borgia is triumphant. Everything has crumbled. What silence! God, have you condemned me? I do not want Hell. I want only to see you, you whose voice I heard.

(*The executioner enters and whips Savonarola.*)

JEROME. You savage!

EXECUTIONER. What? Me a savage?

JEROME. Tell me what savages look like if not like you?

EXECUTIONER. Getting talkative again, eh! During the whipping, all you could do was scream. Now you are giving us a bit of your lip . . .

JEROME. May God forgive you your sins.

EXECUTIONER. I never committed no sins, you lousy misfit. (*whips him*)

JEROME. Barbarian!

EXECUTIONER. Was I a barbarian when I did whippings for you?

JEROME. Did *you* whip them?

EXECUTIONER. You bet your life I did. Here, I'll show you. On behalf of good Brother Jerome, take that, you decadent. And another little lash for the Holy Virgin with the compliments of our good brother who does it simply for your own good.

JEROME. Yes. I had them whipped for their own good. But now, the wicked take their revenge. The whip is no longer the same.

EXECUTIONER. It's the same all right.

JEROME. No.

EXECUTIONER. Don't brush me the wrong way, d'you hear? Where is your good God now, eh?

JEROME. How can you deny God, when you should be the first to believe . . .

EXECUTIONER. Why me?

JEROME. You may whip me again and hear my screams, but if God doesn't hear them too, then nothing has meaning any more. When a naked man is being whipped in the depths of a dungeon, one can sense the presence of God.

EXECUTIONER. I warn you, the whip is just a warm-up. You'll appreciate my skill when I hang you over the fire. I'll try not to strangle you so you can feel the flames licking your feet while you're still alive. I'll see you do a pretty dance — exactly the same job you ordered me to do for the five conspirators in April.

JEROME. I never gave any such order.

EXECUTIONER. Liar. False monk. You ordered them to be burned, didn't you? There was Giannozo Pucci . . . Bernardo del Nero . . . Lorenzo . . . Torna Buoni . . .

JEROME. I asked God to forgive them and ordered them hanged before they were burned.

EXECUTIONER. Oh, I know my job, and I know how to make 'em shout, too. I mix 'em both together. Try to get a delicate balance. And I'm the only one in Florence who can get it exactly right.

Oh, you should have heard how they screamed. Just like you will. "Savage, savage," they shouted, "The monk is mad. We want men to be happy with their wives on this earth," they said. "We want happiness to flourish like a garden under the sun of liberty."

JEROME. They lied. What they called liberty was to sell themselves to the Medicis. I wanted the people to govern themselves under the law of Christ.

EXECUTIONER. I burned them anyway. That's my trade — and I know my trade. Everything depends on the fineness of the knot and the distance of the feet from the fire. Not too high, not too low. Now take an excitable fellow like yourself, I reckon to make you dance four or five minutes. You'll have time to hear them laugh before you die.

JEROME. I shall die tomorrow, but in thirty years you'll all be dead. And thirty years pass so quickly. The Florentine countryside will be just the same, but with other trees and other birds. Men will be living who aren't yet born and some of them will have the same names. In thirty years, all things will be dead and all things living. Everything will be the same and everything different under the unchanging eye of God.

EXECUTIONER. You'll have less to say when I start roasting you. I've seen some of them shouting more from remorse than pain. Oh, you'll hear them laughing at you all right, because you'll look so funny over the fire.

JEROME. Poor wretches. They will still be laughing on earth when I am already with Jesus. (*laughs*)

EXECUTIONER. How can you laugh when you're going to be hanged?

JEROME. Here you are coming back to me, at last. Jesus, you speak to me, you call me. My love.

EXECUTIONER. Your love?

JEROME. Lord Jesus who speaks with me on earth will speak with me tomorrow in Heaven.

EXECUTIONER. Cut out the monkey business.

JEROME. He speaks to me.

EXECUTIONER. What's he say?

106

JEROME. Jesus!

EXECUTIONER. What's he say? Or I'll let you have it.

JEROME. Yes, I was wrong on earth, but what does it matter if I can be right in Heaven.

EXECUTIONER. What's your God saying now?

JEROME. He says he is waiting for me. The madness of the world is dying. God alone is calm. Oh, people of Florence, you think you have deserted me. But it is I who desert you. Hang me quickly, executioner.

EXECUTIONER. I'll hang you tomorrow.

JEROME. Tomorrow? Not till tomorrow? Must I live yet another day among men? I leave you, the living, to grovel in your swill. Henceforth, what does Florence matter to me, or the world, or your crimes and mine? What does my suffering matter? All is comedy and the comedy is over. Know that we are nothing, that what came before us was nothing, that what comes after us will be nothing. All is as nothing. For nothing exists if not you, light of God.

CURTAIN

When the Music Stops

(HISTOIRE DE RIRE)

A PLAY IN THREE ACTS BY
ARMAND SALACROU

ENGLISH VERSION BY NORMAN STOKLE

Characters in Order of Their Appearance

ADELAIDE BARBIER, called "Ade," aged 24

ACHILLES BELLORSON, her lover, aged 23

GERALD BARBIER, Ade's husband, aged 33, a prosperous
businessman

LOUIS DESHAYES, Gerald's friend, aged 31

HELEN DONALDO, Louis' mistress, aged 26

NICOLE, a divorcée of easy virtue, aged 23

JULES DONALDO, Helen's husband, aged 48, an affluent
gravel merchant

The "garret" of the Barbiers' house in Paris. It is a curious room looking out onto a garden. There are two doors, one leading to the other rooms in the house, the other to a balcony. The "garret" is reserved strictly for Gerald, for the mementos of his past, and for his friend, Louis Deshayes, who visits him every evening from six till seven. The "garret" is out of bounds to Ade, Gerald's wife. Despite this, at the rise of the curtain, a trapdoor opens in the floor and Ade appears, looks around, then climbs into the "garret." Then, leaning over the trapdoor, she calls:

ADE. Hurry up, slow-coach.

ACHILLES. (*obviously nervous, following her in*) This is ridiculous.

ADE. So that's how much you love me. (*closes trapdoor*)

ACHILLES. We're heading straight for a catastrophe.

ADE. I hope so.

ACHILLES. But why? Why?

ADE. Because it excites me.

ACHILLES. Oh, you're always the same!

ADE. And you're no longer the same, by the sound of things. You've changed.

ACHILLES. No, I haven't. Really!

ADE. Anyway, I'm not afraid of anything anymore, now you're here.

ACHILLES. But what if your husband came home? What kind of front could I put up? What could I say to him?

ADE. That's why we're here, to find out. Do you expect me to give up everything I own for a few romantic words? I'm leaving my husband and my home, just for you, giving up my servants, my social position, my bed that was made specially to fit me, my Venetian dressing table which is quite unmovable. I'm sacrificing everything, everything, for you. You do love me, Achilles, don't you?

ACHILLES. I'm your lover, aren't I?

ADE. That doesn't prove a thing.

ACHILLES. If I didn't love you, I wouldn't be your lover.

ADE. My adorable pet! You're so refreshing, so wonderfully unsoiled, so different . . .

ACHILLES. This house makes me feel uneasy, especially in here.

ADE. In the garret? It's sacrilege. Except for me, not sacrilege at all, but simply one more proof of my unbounded love for you.

ACHILLES. Haven't I proof already? That afternoon you came to see me and refused me nothing?

ADE. No. Good Heavens!

ACHILLES. No? You mean you can completely surrender yourself without feeling any love?

ADE. Surrender! You couldn't have chosen a better word. Yet to surrender is not to love. Capitulation is not adoration. This very day, I'm not only giving you something I shouldn't, but just by being in the garret, I'm committing a monstrous act. And that's not all.

ACHILLES. (*worried*) Oh Lord, what are you going to do now?

ADE. I don't know yet.

ACHILLES. We both need to calm down a bit.

ADE. No. No. I want to be carried away by it all.

ACHILLES. I'm sorry to feel so uncomfortable like this. But if your husband came in . . .

ADE. How marvelous. Please God let him come in.

ACHILLES. There, now you go calling on God. Take it from me, God wouldn't . . . oh never mind. I'll tell you about Him some other time.

ADE. Could I have been mistaken about you?

ACHILLES. Only one thing concerns me right now . . . how to stop this damned perspiration. I'm in a cold sweat.

112

ADE. My poor pet, I understand. Achilles, just think, my husband won't even let me look inside his darling little garret. But here I am. And you too. Ah, if you only knew how he raves about "his garret." He and Louis irritate me no end with their garret worship. Do you know Louis? They've been friends since they were running around in short pants.

ACHILLES. Oh?

ADE. A friendship without precedent and still as strong as ever.

ACHILLES. Really!

ADE. Darling, sit down. Try to relax. (*Achilles sits, then stands up again.*) They've been trying to recapture their childhood memories for years now. See this wicker hamper? Gerald hid himself inside it at his Aunt Ada's when he was four years old, so it's been rotting away here ever since. And Gerald's no spring chicken. He's well over thirty. It wouldn't surprise me if they played hide and seek in it. They are mad, the pair of them. And you know, my pet, they come here every day at six o'clock on the dot.

ACHILLES. So that's why you are always free at six.

ADE. Yes. And here, any business talk is absolutely taboo, as my husband is such an important businessman.

ACHILLES. I know.

ADE. Louis too. In advertising. He invents things which help sell other things which other people invent . . . anyway it's some kind of business. Well, in here, no business, no politics, or so I gather . . . they never include me in their ridiculous games . . . oh, and no telephone.

ACHILLES. (*sincerely*) Sounds wonderful.

ADE. Not even a clock. Their watches they leave outside.

ACHILLES. Do they always come in by that door?

ADE. Sometimes through the garden.

ACHILLES. But never before six?

ADE. Very rarely.

ACHILLES. (*anxiously*) It's a quarter to.

ADE. Then at seven, Joseph, our servant, rings the bell for the end of their playtime. (*pointing to a billiard table*) Louis bought this old thing from a café in the Latin quarter. They used to play on

113

it when they were at college together. Do you know how to play, darling?

ACHILLES. Very badly.

ADE. Then I'll teach you. Give me some money.

ACHILLES. What if your husband comes in and catches us? His private billiard table with all the memories of his youth? I love you, Ade, but that doesn't prevent me from respecting your husband.

ADE. I should hope not! Do you imagine I could love you if you didn't respect him? The man whose name I share? And how could I love him if he wasn't worthy of respect?

ACHILLES. There, you see, you still love your husband.

ADE. Of course I love Gerald. And I'm happy to love him because that makes my sacrifice for you much greater.

ACHILLES. Anything you say, only don't tell him about it.

ADE. How do you expect me to leave my husband without him finding out?

ACHILLES. It's obviously very difficult for you.

ADE. What's the matter? Are you jealous, my pet? How silly you are. I promise you my husband is no more than an old friend.

ACHILLES. It's five to six.

ADE. Go and wait for me in the garden.

ACHILLES. Is it straight down? Could I lose my way?

ADE. Wait for me by the weeping rosebush.

ACHILLES. (*going quickly*) Very well, but if we don't see each other again this evening, I'll call you as usual tomorrow morning.

ADE. Wait for me, Achilles.

ACHILLES. (*subdued*) How long?

ADE. Until I get there.

ACHILLES. Oh, all right (*pitifully*) . . . my dearest. (*moves to exit*)

ADE. Come and kiss me. (*They kiss.*) Oh, my head spins. An unforgettable giddiness . . .

ACHILLES. By the weeping rosebush . . . (*runs out to the garden*)

ADE. (*looking at a large picture of herself*) My unframed photograph, my last remembrance for you, dear Gerald, all ready to

114

be torn into little pieces. How pathetic, a man's fingers tearing up the photo of his loved one. Oh, how I'd love to be here to see you torturing yourself. Poor Gerald. (*to photo*) I wonder how he'll tear me up? Sadly, angrily, shouting his head off, or crying his eyes out? Oh, how you will cry, Gerald.

(*She puts out the light. Gerald enters through the trapdoor, lights up the garret, looks at a tobacco container, then sees his wife.*)

GERALD. (*flabbergasted*) What the devil are you doing here?

ADE. (*pathetically*) Gerald!

GERALD. (*furious*) Who gave you permission to come in here?

ADE. Gerald, I can still remember the day you first kissed me and you said, "I'm very serious about this, I intend to marry you," and your eyes were full of tears.

GERALD. Ade, you're being a nuisance, dear.

ADE. Gerald, I have something serious to ask you, very serious. And I need an answer urgently. Do you love me more than anything else in the world? If I were to die . . .

GERALD. My dear Ade, you're in perfect health. Now, off you go into the garden for a while. It'll give you an appetite for dinner.

ADE. Into the garden? Into the garden! That's not even funny. Or maybe it's fate speaking to me. But I'm asking you, Gerald, not fate. If I were to disappear from the world, or from your life . . .

GERALD. Disappear from my life? I'm not asking you to do that; I just want you to take a breath of fresh air and leave me alone here with Louis until seven. Is that beyond your strength?

ADE. And have you great strength?

GERALD. Why? Do I have to throw you out by force?

ADE. Well, this simplifies things tremendously. For if I am not mistaken, you no longer love me?

GERALD. You know I do, Ade. Now look, I am worn out with work. Work I no longer enjoy. One of my few remaining pleasures is to meet here with Louis every evening for one hour of perfect peace and quiet.

ADE. What do you discuss? Who do you talk about?

GERALD. What? Who? Nothing! That's the whole point, my dear little Ade. We don't talk about anything.

ADE. Ade, dear little Ade . . . always Ade. Well, I'm not your dear little Ade any longer. I'm sick and tired of being your dear little Ade. My name is Adelaide. I have the blood of 1830 in my veins. Yes, me, do you hear? I have ancestors going back to the revolution of 1830.

GERALD. So have I.

ADE. You? You? That's funny.

GERALD. My dear Ade, everyone living today had ancestors living in 1830. You and me like everyone else.

ADE. It's not true. You're trying to humiliate me again.

GERALD. If you think for just one second, perhaps your day will not have been entirely wasted. Everyone living today has ancestors who lived in every century since the world was created.

ADE. You're mad. How can you believe . . . why yes . . . of course. It's strange when you think about it. Anyway, my great-grandmother was called Adelaide, not dear little Ade.

GERALD. Yes, and she had love affairs with every Tom, Dick, and Harry she laid eyes on.

ADE. She was the loving kind.

GERALD. Many women, Ade, mistakenly equate their few little nervous crises with the life of a great lover.

ADE. Of course, you know what love really is?

GERALD. For a woman, true love means loving a man from the beginning of her life to the end, through every phase of her existence. (*sees photo*) What's that?

ADE. Don't tear it up, don't tear it up . . . not yet.

GERALD. Take that photograph and put it back in my room.

ADE. No. I want it to stay here.

GERALD. You're infuriating.

ADE. So, you're trying to forget me in this precious little garret of yours?

GERALD. Yes.

ADE. But you don't try to forget the other women you have known,

116

do you? Because you had this armchair before we were married. All your stupid mistresses must have sat in it.

GERALD. Will you be quiet.

ADE. And your uncle's hunting gun. The one with the shapely daughter! Just a "cousin." Oh yes!

GERALD. Ade!

ADE. (*upsetting all the objects*) And this rare edition of Bossuet's *Funeral Orations* that you sold to buy a pink satin dress for some bitch in the Latin quarter. Then Louis found it on a quayside stall and bought it back for your garret.

GERALD. I shall have to shut you up.

ADE. If I were sure you'd strangle me out of love, I'd keep on going. But what's the use?

GERALD. I certainly wouldn't strangle you, Ade, because all you deserve is a good box on the ears like a spoilt brat.

ADE. Boor! You boorish boor! My horrible, hateful husband! The man I've sacrificed all my dreams for, for the past six years. Oh! All my youth wasted on this brute. My grandmother must be laughing her head off up there.

GERALD. Up there! Or down below! Why not down below?

ADE. Monster. You'd see my grandmother in Hell, wouldn't you. You repulsive beast.

GERALD. Get the hell out of here.

ADE. That's the only way you know how to speak.

GERALD. Don't force me to throw you out.

ADE. No. But since I at least have a certain refinement, please ask me again to go into the garden.

GERALD. The garden or somewhere else, but not here.

ADE. First, I'll go into the garden, then somewhere else. (*She laughs. Louis enters.*)

LOUIS. Well, we don't seem to be having too boring a time.

ADE. I notice Louis doesn't immediately go off the handle because I'm here.

GERALD. Give him time.

LOUIS. So, it wasn't really laughter I heard, only the outward appearance.

117

ADE. I'll leave you now. On my husband's orders, I'm going into the garden to find a purpose for life!

GERALD. I've never known her to be so maddening.

ADE. I'm sorry to have disturbed your little recreation for the first time in six years, Louis. However, I shall have to disturb you once again.

GERALD. I absolutely forbid it.

LOUIS. What's going on?

GERALD. Look, old man, ask anything except questions. Otherwise she'll sit and tell us her little stories till seven o'clock.

ADE. And my little stories don't interest you. You prefer your ridiculous little games to my stories.

GERALD. If we are friendly, she'll come back tomorrow with flowers, the day after with tea and cakes. By the end of the week, we'll have had just about enough to move out.

ADE. Don't worry, Louis. After meditating a little by the weeping rosebush, I'd like to have a few words with you, just for five minutes, about a very serious matter. Please don't refuse.

LOUIS. Is it so serious?

ADE. Decisive! A rare opportunity for a heart-moving conversation. Help me not to miss it. (*to Gerald*) I'm going to question fate by the weeping rosebush.

GERALD. Don't worry on my account. I shan't disturb you.

ADE. As you wish, but I repeat, I shall be near the weeping rosebush. You might find my situation rather interesting.

GERALD. Very good! And get rid of this photograph. (*picks it up*)

ADE. Louis, don't let him tear it up. Listen, Gerald, if you tear it up now, you'll be sorry before the evening's over. Or else, don't make the pieces too small so you have enough left over to tear into smaller pieces later on.

LOUIS. (*with charm*) My dear Ade . . .

ADE. When we have our chat, your dear Ade may surprise you more than you think. Count on me, Louis. (*exits*)

LOUIS. What novel has she been reading today?

GERALD. I don't know.

LOUIS. Has she been to a film?

118

GERALD. I don't think so.

LOUIS. I wonder where she read about tearing up the photograph.

GERALD. Look, Ade is my wife, and you are kind not to tell me what you think of her, but don't mince words with me. She's a damned nuisance. I want you to make it perfectly clear to her that she might have waited until dinner before having this romantic little tête-à-tête. (*angrily*) Why the devil couldn't she have waited until seven?

LOUIS. I don't know.

GERALD. And you should have told her: fine, Ade, anything you like, but after seven o'clock.

LOUIS. It's just that I've an appointment at seven.

GERALD. Oh marvelous! You're sure you can wait that long?

LOUIS. Oh yes . . . of course. Besides, Ade will have forgotten all about that decisive conversation by then.

GERALD. (*playing billiards*) Hmm. The great psychologist. And now, not another word about her. Your turn.

LOUIS. (*reluctant*) Gerald . . .

GERALD. What?

LOUIS. (*preparing to play*) Nothing.

GERALD. (*thinking Louis is trying to cheat by distracting him*) Oh, congratulations. Why don't you push the balls with your fingers. It would be more honest.

LOUIS. I'm sorry. But I don't feel up to cheating today.

GERALD. (*unbelieving smile*) Really!

LOUIS. I don't even feel like playing.

GERALD. (*continuing to play*) Is this some sort of new ploy? Pulling a fast one on your opponent by refusing to play?

LOUIS. No, Gerald. I feel more like talking.

GERALD. Go ahead. Talk.

LOUIS. What I have to say should really wait until seven, if we followed the rules. But I'd rather tell you immediately.

GERALD. Oh no, not now, old man. Not now.

LOUIS. All right, then. I'll wait.

GERALD. First it's Ade, and now your personal problems. I mean,

119

we're not here to waste our time. We've managed to salvage one hour a day to live. And I'm hanging on to it. Play.

LOUIS. Yes, Gerald.

GERALD. (*very friendly*) Was it to do with some outside business?

LOUIS. (*to Gerald who is playing darts*) Stop throwing darts on my very first bowler hat. I'm in no laughing mood today.

GERALD. (*seeing Louis looking at his watch*) Are you out of your mind? You're still wearing your watch.

LOUIS. Listen . . .

GERALD. Go and put that thing downstairs, first. For Heaven's sake, Louis! The fetter of time! Time! Watching us, always watching us from morning till night, and you hold on to it!

LOUIS. Gerald, listen to me.

GERALD. We're imprisoned, confined like rabbits in hutches. "Eleven o'clock? Ask my eleven o'clock appointment to come in. Eleven-fifteen? Next client please. Eleven-thirty? Next client. Twelve? Next. Next. What? Five to one already? And I'm lunching with the president at one." Oh, God!

LOUIS. Gerald . . . (*Gerald blows into a hunting horn. Louis shouts*) Gerald. (*then, earnestly*) I love a woman.

GERALD. What?

LOUIS. Oh Lord, how stupid that sounds. I don't mean any woman. I mean her . . . she . . . I am in love, and she is my love.

GERALD. She? Who?

LOUIS. Oh, my dear fellow, wait till you see her. My dream woman. My only woman. As if I could love anyone else. I've met the woman of my life, my woman for eternity.

GERALD. When? Today?

LOUIS. No.

GERALD. Yesterday?

LOUIS. No. Two and a half years ago.

GERALD. (*laughing at this "joke" in the true "garret tradition"*) Full marks. Ten out of ten. Ha! Ha! Two and a half . . . ha! ha!

LOUIS. I'm not fooling. This is no joke.

GERALD. Is she a young virgin?

LOUIS. No.

120

GERALD. A widow?

LOUIS. No.

GERALD. Divorced?

LOUIS. Not yet.

GERALD. A married woman!

LOUIS. Yes. And we've been seeing each other practically every day for the past two and a half years.

GERALD. Every day? And this is the first I've heard of it?

LOUIS. I'm only telling you now, because she's decided to leave her husband today. I asked her to come and meet me here at seven so I could introduce her to you and Ade, and the garret.

GERALD. It seems she knows all about the garret, even if I don't know her.

LOUIS. Well, this garret isn't exactly easy to hide from a woman. After all, we've been coming here every night for God knows how long. To begin with, she thought it was one of my old mistresses.

GERALD. That she wanted you to give up?

LOUIS. No. But at first, she thought I loved her, and I thought she loved me. And that was enough for both of us.

GERALD. And you've kept me in the dark about her for two and a half years — about someone you'd only just left or were going to see.

LOUIS. Our rules prevented any sort of outside discussion.

GERALD. So this Aphrodite who means more than heaven and earth to you remained a stranger to our garret.

LOUIS. As I said, I thought at first it was just another affair like all the rest, then one that was having a long run. That was my only reason for saying nothing about it before now.

GERALD. Where did you meet this woman?

LOUIS. This woman!

GERALD. What do you expect me to say? I don't know her name.

LOUIS. Helen.

GERALD. (*trying several tones of voice*) Helen . . . Helen . . . Helen . . . (*shouts*) Helen.

LOUIS. What's the matter?

GERALD. I'll be hearing the name for the rest of my life, having it in my mouth and ears every day. So, at the very start, I listen to it, murmur it, shout it, look at it. Helen. I feel it . . . Helen . . . It's charming. Not bad at all. Where did you meet this Helen?

LOUIS. In an accident coming into town, on a very confusing cloverleaf. She's an excellent driver.

GERALD. An excellent driver? And she bumped into you?

LOUIS. Yes, she did. Well, aren't you happy for me?

GERALD. Frankly, I'm disappointed. We being such close friends and you never saying a word about it. You know I never keep anything from you.

LOUIS. I'm the secretive type, I suppose?

GERALD. You've told me now, all right, but . . .

LOUIS. I couldn't tell you yesterday.

GERALD. Why not?

LOUIS. Because I didn't know myself.

GERALD. Didn't know what?

LOUIS. That she'd be leaving her husband today.

GERALD. Does he know the horrible truth?

LOUIS. No. Not yet. He's an old man, anyway, twenty years older than she is. Little more than a friend, really. In fact, that's all he's been to her for ages.

GERALD. So she decided to make the break.

LOUIS. No. It's like this. Her husband left for Holland a week ago on a business trip that should have lasted two weeks. She told some tale or other to her servants at home and we went to stay at a quiet little hotel in the country. We were just starting to enjoy ourselves, when he wired this morning to say he'd finished his business and was coming home right away. I hated the idea of her going back tonight and it was more than she could bear after living with me. Then suddenly we realized we'd both been passionately in love all these years and that we simply couldn't live apart. If her husband had come home at the proper time, when we'd arranged to separate, we might never have realized. She's writing him a note at the moment. Then she's coming here at seven.

122

GERALD. Is this the first time you've lived together?

LOUIS. No. We spent the winter vacation together at Mégève.

GERALD. Oh yes! You discovered the joys of skiing . . . I remember.

LOUIS. It was wonderful, having breakfast with her, and dancing in the evening.

GERALD. But you still managed to let her go when you came back.

LOUIS. Yes, because we'd arranged it that way. But today, when she got the telegram, she said to me, "What a pity. If only he didn't have to come back."

GERALD. (*without conviction*) Poor man.

LOUIS. You should pity her, too.

GERALD. Pity her?

LOUIS. Leaving him will cause the dickens of a scandal. She's quite a leading light, socially.

GERALD. Divorce is as respectable as marriage, nowadays.

LOUIS. Helen has money of her own. That should make things easier. And her husband is worth a mint. He's a pretty important man in his field.

GERALD. What does he do?

LOUIS. He sells stones. He's the biggest gravel and stone merchant in Paris.

GERALD. Donaldo? (*laughs*)

LOUIS. You know him?

GERALD. He has a charming wife.

LOUIS. You know her?

GERALD. No. I've met Donaldo and his wife only two or three times.

LOUIS. What does he look like?

GERALD. My memory of him is rather hazy . . . I shouldn't recognize him again. Haven't you ever met him?

LOUIS. Never. Of course, I've often heard about him. But I've gone out of my way to avoid meeting him.

GERALD. Why?

LOUIS. Firstly out of consideration for him.

GERALD. (*ironically*) Damn decent of you, old man! And when will he learn the good news?

LOUIS. He's arriving on the "North Star" express tonight.

GERALD. Don't feel too sorry for him. He probably has a mistress himself.

LOUIS. Don't let Helen hear you say that, please. I suggested the same thing once, and she took it very badly.

GERALD. And at the time, you were both . . . er . . . in your pajamas?

LOUIS. (*smiling*) Yes.

GERALD. Ah!

LOUIS. Gerald, you don't know how relieved I am. I was afraid you'd think badly of me.

GERALD. Why?

LOUIS. Because I'm giving grounds for divorce, and in the meantime imposing Helen on you and Ade.

GERALD. You grieve me, Louis. Not only are you secretive, but you seem to think six years of marriage have made me unfit to understand the most commonplace situations.

LOUIS. The most commonplace . . .

GERALD. Don't fancy yourself as some great criminal just because your mistress is a married woman. It's quite a widespread occupation. Have you forgotten our college days?

LOUIS. (*reticent*) No.

GERALD. Now if you had been a real friend, you'd have asked me to call on Donaldo long ago. I'd have liked that. Cuckolds always say the funniest things.

LOUIS. I stopped telling you about my love life when you got married out of respect for Ade and so as not to upset your faithful peace of mind.

GERALD. Don't tell me you kept up the crazy life we led together?

LOUIS. I kept on, just as when you were around. All pickups were fair game and didn't last long. The darlings would say they loved me — which was all the same to me — and I would say I adored them out of politeness. Then one day, along came Helen. It began like all the rest but this time it was different.

GERALD. Well, I must say, when I met the Donaldos a couple of years ago, the delightful Helen betrayed no sign of adultery.

124

LOUIS. Adultery is a big word. She married stupidly without being in love, like a lot of girls. I was her first affair, her first lover. Don't reproach her tonight for having a lover. I can count on you, can't I?

GERALD. Of course.

LOUIS. What about Ade?

GERALD. (*anxiously*) You know her. She's quite capable of putting on the Christian marriage act and asking Helen about the prospects of a papal annulment. Or else she could be deeply moved by it all and compare Helen with her grandmother Adelaide — which wouldn't help things in the slightest.

LOUIS. I gently prepared Helen.

GERALD. (*aggressively*) For what?

LOUIS. For Ade's spontaneity, her refreshing spirit, her charming, impulsive romanticism.

GERALD. But you still have misgivings?

LOUIS. What do you think?

GERALD. When you have this "decisive conversation," turn on your inimitable charm and tell her how happy you are.

LOUIS. Thanks, Gerald. You're a real friend.

GERALD. I've had the same happiness myself, I envy you. You bring back those wonderful times I knew with Ade, when we suddenly realized we were in love. Everybody talks about love but you have to discover it for yourself to really understand . . . (*Enter Ade.*)

ADE. You're going to keep your promise, aren't you, Louis?

LOUIS. Of course, Ade.

GERALD. (*to Ade*) Five minutes and no more. I'll wait in the hall . . . (*to Louis*) where I left my watch.

ADE. Gerald, look at me. There must be a word, a phrase to preserve this moment forever in your memory.

GERALD. You're right, Louis. She is reading a novel.

ADE. What a pity! There won't be any last word.

GERALD. Oh yes, my dear little Ade. You are so enchanting yet so tempestuous. (*exits by trapdoor*)

125

ADE. Poor Gerald. (*to Louis*) What sort of woman would you say I was?

LOUIS. The charming wife of my best friend.

ADE. Gerald thinks I'm tempestuous and you think I'm Gerald's wife. You are both idiots, the pair of you.

LOUIS. Very good.

ADE. I'm classified and labeled like a jar in a museum that nobody looks at. And now and again, I'm dusted by the old custodian for something to do. (*picks up a small bowler hat*)

LOUIS. Don't touch that hat. It means a lot to me. My grandfather bought it for me when I was ten years old for my cousin's first communion. I hated wearing it, I looked so ridiculous. My mother thought so, too, but it made grandfather happy. It's a relic, you see, a symbol. (*He moves to take the hat. Ade throws it on the floor.*)

ADE. Louis, look at me. Do you know I have already been unfaithful to Gerald five times?

LOUIS. (*unbelievingly*) With the same man or five different ones?

ADE. I'm in love, Louis, madly in love. And I don't mean Gerald. Don't look so uncomfortable, it's not you either.

LOUIS. I'm disappointed, and delighted. I abhor dramatic situations.

ADE. How sad! Because tonight I want you to tell Gerald I've already had five lovers.

LOUIS. Me? I hate spreading gossip.

ADE. This isn't gossip. It's a message.

LOUIS. Why ask me to do it?

ADE. Because it will help Gerald to bear the rest . . .

LOUIS. The rest? What does the next chapter say?

ADE. Don't be so sarcastic.

LOUIS. What have you been reading? Casanova?

ADE. Aren't I capable of being loved?

LOUIS. (*seriously*) Gerald worships you.

ADE. Stop confusing me. I won't be sidetracked. Louis, I'm leaving Gerald.

LOUIS. What are you saying?

126

ADE. I'm leaving with no luggage, no jewelry, and no regrets.

LOUIS. What is this? Some silly joke?

ADE. And I'm leaving now. You are Gerald's friend, so you will comfort and console him.

LOUIS. You want me to tell Gerald you've left him.

ADE. If you want your best friend to run around all night from one police station to the next and telephone all the hospitals in Paris, that's your privilege. You know Gerald hates worry of any kind. I leave the matter in your hands.

LOUIS. But this is impossible. Are you out of your mind?

ADE. Would you rather I be cruel and tell him myself, or leave him a note?

LOUIS. A note? A note! Dear God! This is ridiculous.

ADE. You think my love is ridiculous?

LOUIS. Your love? What love? Don't try and tell me you have a lover.

ADE. Why not? I'm a perfectly normal woman.

LOUIS. But you were so close to each other. I've talked with you, had meals with you. We've all been to parties together . . .

ADE. Did you expect me to confide in any friend of Gerald's?

LOUIS. But you always spoke so lovingly to each other. How could you possibly have been seeing another man?

ADE. When a woman says goodnight to her lover, it doesn't mean she should start beating her husband when she gets home.

LOUIS. You're insane.

ADE. If you think I'm insane, I wonder what sort of women you associate with?

LOUIS. All this business must have some ulterior motive. You've obviously heard something about me and invented this ridiculous joke?

ADE. I don't follow you.

LOUIS. Please tell me the truth.

ADE. I never lie.

LOUIS. You must have lied to Gerald.

ADE. I've never lied to him. Never.

LOUIS. Did you tell him you had one lover, or half a dozen?

127

ADE. He didn't ask me. I never had to lie to him.

LOUIS. What about lying by omission?

ADE. There's no point in wasting your time teaching me the various methods of lying. I simply ask you to tell Gerald the truth this evening.

LOUIS. Have you really thought thoroughly about . . .

ADE. And it's equally pointless giving me a lecture on morality.

LOUIS. But you can't walk out on Gerald like this.

ADE. Because he's your friend?

LOUIS. He also happens to be your husband.

ADE. And don't start preaching about the sacred bonds of matrimony.

LOUIS. Why not?

ADE. Oh, very well, go ahead. I'm all ears.

LOUIS. (*after an uneasy silence*) Well, er . . . Gerald loves you . . .

ADE. So does Achilles.

LOUIS. Achilles! So that's his name.

ADE. Now perhaps you'll believe I'm not joking.

LOUIS. You sound almost proud of deceiving Gerald.

ADE. No. Only happy.

LOUIS. You imagine yourself a heroine in some novel or other. But there's nothing exceptional in having a lover these days. So many women are unfaithful, it's becoming tedious. True love is the rare thing today.

ADE. I love Achilles. That's why I'm going to spend the rest of my life with him.

LOUIS. How can I tell you . . .

ADE. How Gerald will suffer?

LOUIS. Yes. Think of Gerald's feelings when he hears you've deceived him. He'll break his heart.

ADE. Tut! Tut! Dear little Ade!

LOUIS. Proud of yourself, too! Doesn't even the thought of Gerald's suffering hold you back?

ADE. In the first place, if I don't leave, he won't suffer.

LOUIS. But if you do . . .

128

ADE. It's either Gerald or Achilles. One of them has to suffer. I have to choose. And since I love Achilles, I prefer to let Gerald do the suffering.

LOUIS. Listen, I'll arrange everything. God help me, I'll have to. The alternative's unthinkable. Leave everything to me. Say nothing to Gerald. Tell me where this person is and I'll go and see him myself. Anything to avoid a catastrophe. I'll tell him you haven't changed your mind, but that some unforeseeable hitch . . . anyway, I'll tell him that tomorrow morning you'll . . . I promise I'll find something to keep him happy. He won't suffer. And Gerald will still have a pleasant evening.

ADE. And what about my evening? My only joy is to be with my lover. You're forgetting that.

LOUIS. The word "lover" is pure poetry to you, isn't it? Ade, marriage and love are not necessarily irreconcilable. You loved Gerald once. Think again. In your position, a divorce . . .

ADE. Oh! We agree for the first time. The word "divorce" is not poetic. (*Gerald appears through the trapdoor.*) It has a bad ring to it. Divorce. If the word hadn't existed, it would probably have been invented by surgeons to denote a new tumor. "This poor woman is not at all well. Oh! What's the trouble? She has a divorce!"

GERALD. Just as I thought.

ADE. You were listening?

GERALD. I heard enough.

ADE. I did want to avoid the scene of a wife deserting her husband.

GERALD. For Heaven's sake, Ade! Helen Donaldo is a fine woman.

LOUIS. (*to Gerald*) Gerald, please. Give us another minute. Just one more minute.

GERALD. You are far too indulgent with this crazy woman. Divorce! The name of a tumor! When a woman no longer loves her husband, she not only has the right but the duty to leave him and join the man she loves.

LOUIS. Gerald!

ADE. (*aside to Louis*) The shock! It's gone to his head.

GERALD. Louis loves Helen — you see, I'm calling her Helen already — and Helen loves Louis. Simplicity itself. They've been in love for two and a half years, but out of respect for us, they were discreet about it. Now, they've decided to go off together, and Louis has invited Helen to dine with us this evening — and quite right too. Tell Joseph to prepare one more place at table.

ADE. I've finished giving orders to Joseph.

GERALD. (*to Ade*) Damn it all, haven't we often talked about Louis getting married some day. About the sort of woman he would bring here? You know Helen Donaldo's reputation as well as I do. You should be happy for Louis, happy he's chosen Helen Donaldo to be our friend.

ADE. Is Mrs. Donaldo your mistress?

GERALD. Call her Helen, and forget the commentary.

ADE. Is she deserting her husband for you?

GERALD. "Deserting her husband." How you dramatize everything. Instead of returning to her husband tonight, she'll stay with Louis, that's all.

ADE. That's all.

GERALD. That's all. The lawyers will straighten things out afterwards.

ADE. This is extremely interesting. Have you a good lawyer, Louis?

GERALD. How infuriating you are sometimes. I'll start swearing in a minute.

ADE. Oh, for Heaven's sake . . .

LOUIS. Gerald, leave me alone with Ade.

GERALD. So you can start arguing all over again? No.

ADE. Correct me if I'm wrong, but Mrs. Donaldo is leaving the husband she's been deceiving for the past two and a half years . . .

GERALD. I approve of Helen, do you hear?

ADE. For taking a lover?

GERALD. And I suspect you approve of her too.

ADE. For deceiving her husband?

GERALD. Tell Joseph to lay another place.

ADE. But this morning you told me . . .

GERALD. I've changed my mind.

130

ADE. Let's hope you won't change your mind again in five minutes.

LOUIS. Gerald . . .

GERALD. Quiet. Ade's the one who's always talking about love. She should at least try to understand you and Helen.

ADE. I find your attitude surprising, disturbing. Because if I follow you correctly, when a woman no longer loves her husband, she has the right to deceive him; and no one should blame her for it, not even the husband. Am I right?

LOUIS. Gerald . . .

GERALD. Quiet. (*to Ade*) In certain cases, yes.

ADE. Such as?

LOUIS. Gerald . . .

ADE. Louis, I think you'll agree that Gerald's answer is of extreme interest.

GERALD. (*to Louis*) All right. Let me handle this. (*to Ade*) Your grandmother made love into a parlor game, a sort of bedroom version of musical chairs.

ADE. Yes, I know. Just like Messalina, Catherine the Great, and . . .

GERALD. But when a woman loves a man to the point of sacrificing everything for him . . . (*bursting*) You're forever mentioning Tristan and Isolde when you complain about me reading the *Debates Journal* and *The Times* every night. But you forget, my dear little Ade, that even Isolde was unfaithful to her husband.

LOUIS. That's enough. It's not Ade I want to talk to any more. It's you, Gerald. (*to Ade*) And you stay here.

ADE. Just a minute, Louis.

GERALD. Let him speak.

ADE. What time is Helen Donaldo arriving?

GERALD. Seven.

ADE. Ha! Don't count on it.

GERALD. What do you know about it?

ADE. In the first place, she could be late.

GERALD. Oh!

ADE. But she may not even come.

GERALD. You are looking for trouble again.

131

ADE. Her husband might win her back at the last minute, Louis.

GERALD. You are wasting your malicious breath. She has enough tact and decency to leave without making a fuss. She won't see her husband.

ADE. Perhaps she'll ask one of her husband's friends to break the news — and he'll oblige in the name of morality . . . no not morality, he wouldn't have the nerve . . . in the name of friendship.

GERALD. (*to Louis*) Don't let her delirious imagination put you off.

LOUIS. To tell you the truth, Gerald . . .

ADE. Let me finish, Louis. I'm intrigued by this friend of Helen's.

GERALD. There isn't any friend. There'll just be a note.

ADE. The friend speaks to the husband, tells him everything, then at the last minute, this woman . . .

GERALD. For God's sake stop saying "this woman." Her name is Helen.

ADE. . . . changes her mind and decides not to leave. But the friend's message, announcing a desertion that never happens, might well provoke another that does.

LOUIS. You think she won't leave him?

GERALD. (*to Ade*) Helen will leave her husband. Rest assured of that.

ADE. Fortunately.

GERALD. At last. Ade's becoming human.

ADE. How pitiful it would be if she stayed. Her husband would see her again in the evening, just like any other evening without knowing how close he had been to losing her. He would have brushed misfortune aside by his ordinary everyday gestures. How dreadfully comic!

GERALD. She's so right. Just like in some of those old films . . .

ADE. Yes. The hole in the sidewalk. (*to Gerald*) You remember? The man doesn't see it . . . He's going to fall in . . . no . . . he moves back . . . he moves forward . . . and passes it very calmly without seeing a thing.

GERALD. But Donaldo will fall right into it! (*laughs*)

ADE. And he laughs. (*Ade and Louis exchange glances.*)

GERALD. Yes. I can just see the look on Donaldo's face when he finds out. Ha! ha!

ADE. (*indignant*) Oh, don't be so coarse, Gerald.

LOUIS. (*to Ade*) It's shameful.

(*Ade bursts out laughing.*)

GERALD. What are you laughing for?

ADE. (*to Louis*) It'd be so funny if instead of announcing Helen, Joseph ushered in her friend, all pale and drawn, to tell you she had changed her mind . . .

GERALD. Don't start again, Ade.

ADE. What a wonderful night that would be!

GERALD. How vile you are!

ADE. Do you think I'm vile, Louis? What would you say to her friend?

LOUIS. (*near breaking point*) If leaving her husband will cause such distress, I hope to Heaven she stays home, at least for tonight.

GERALD. Don't be influenced by Ade. (*to Ade*) You are monstrous. (*to Louis*) Forgive her, my dear fellow . . .

LOUIS. I'll forgive her if . . .

ADE. I'm sorry, Louis. Look at me. Don't you see, I've been teasing you.

LOUIS. I'm still a little dazed.

ADE. How can you take all my imaginings so seriously?

GERALD. Let's not say another word about it.

ADE. Agreed.

GERALD. And you approve of Helen?

ADE. Completely.

GERALD. (*to Louis*) What more could you want?

LOUIS. Oh, shut up. You're just making things worse.

ADE. (*to Louis*) Because we've made our peace!

GERALD. I fail to see how I make things worse by asking her to approve of Helen.

LOUIS. Please! (*to Ade*) You and your devilish ideas . . . How could you imagine . . . I feel like kissing and striking you at the same time.

133

GERALD. That would certainly make things worse — striking Ade just when she's becoming reasonable.

ADE. My dear Louis, I'm grieved that you could believe what I've just said.

LOUIS. Oh, I've acted like a child.

GERALD. Like a man in love, my friend.

ADE. Believing Helen wouldn't come. Or telling her husband to phone and say she'd be spending the night with him instead of you. Really! How ridiculous.

LOUIS. If you're teasing me, Ade, please stop. I can't take it any more.

GERALD. (to Louis) I don't understand you.

ADE. Helen will keep her appointment. Trust my feminine intuition.

GERALD. Ade has talent.

LOUIS. (disheveled) What?

GERALD. (to Ade) I say, you have talent. Ade understands a woman's heart. And you also approve of Helen not telling her husband herself, don't you? (to Louis) Don't be so depressed. Why force her to tell her husband to his face that she no longer loves him? It's grotesque.

ADE. Grotesque!

GERALD. And not very clever, either. If he still loves his wife, he'll be even more upset. The confession becomes a sort of death penalty. He'll fight desperately for his cause like a drowning man clutching at a straw.

ADE. So enjoy your happiness while you have it. Don't spoil this rare moment. A woman is so happy going to meet the man she loves.

LOUIS. If you are not completely mad . . .

GERALD. Why insult Ade when she's being so agreeable?

ADE. Forget your scruples. Nothing in the world can hold her back.

LOUIS. In the name of our friendship . . .

ADE. Mad or not, I'm only sorry I won't be here this evening. The first time there's a little excitement in this house I have to miss it.

GERALD. (to Louis) Why is she mad? (to Ade) And why won't

you be here this evening? You're not going to start your squabbling all over again, are you?

ADE. If I stayed, there'd be no excitement. And I'd merely envy the courage of a woman who herself had not hesitated. Gerald, look at me. Goodbye.

GERALD. (*to Louis*) Why did you call her mad?

LOUIS. (*to Ade*) Move one step and I'll tell him everything.

GERALD. What?

ADE. Didn't I say you'd tell him? Oh how I'd love to hear your conversation in five minutes' time. But if I stayed, you wouldn't say it. So I'm going. Good luck. (*laughs and goes out into the garden*)

GERALD. Where is she going?

LOUIS. Ade!

GERALD. Everything was fine. If only you had . . .

LOUIS. Everything wasn't fine. She made fools of us, the little bitch! But please, please go and bring her back. Ade! Ade!

GERALD. Where has she gone?

LOUIS. Run after her, for Heaven's sake. Use force, but stop her!

GERALD. She shouldn't have teased you like that. It was stupid of her, but you know my wife. Anyway, with you on your honeymoon, you might have been a little less touchy.

LOUIS. Poor Gerald.

GERALD. I didn't expect such a stormy outburst from you, or such clumsiness. Ade has the excitement of a child, but she's a good, honest, straightforward girl.

LOUIS. Oooh! (*tries to tear up Ade's photo*)

GERALD. Here, you're not going to tear up her photograph?

LOUIS. (*failing to do so*) She's stuck it onto some cloth. It won't tear, the bitch!

GERALD. Not that I'm offended, but I've never heard you call my wife that before.

LOUIS. Poor Gerald.

GERALD. Pity me if it makes you feel any better, but in spite of appearances, I'm not sorry to be Ade's husband.

LOUIS. Ade's husband!

135

GERALD. Now simmer down and tell me, what sort of personality has Helen?

LOUIS. Her personality . . .

GERALD. Is it sweet, calm, aggressive?

LOUIS. Why?

GERALD. If Ade behaves like that at dinner, will Helen give her as much as she gets, or will she try to charm her?

LOUIS. Helen? What's the time? (*looks at watch*) Oh! (*pause*) I've just had a terrifying thought.

GERALD. Stop worrying. Helen will be here.

LOUIS. I don't doubt it. I had planned for us to talk about something quite different until seven; then I should have left with Helen.

GERALD. Don't you want to have dinner with us this evening?

LOUIS. I can't leave you like this. I must stay with you.

GERALD. You're upset, Louis. Don't hide anything from me. I heard her goading you as I came in about Helen's divorce. What nasty things did she come out with before then?

LOUIS. Nasty isn't the word.

GERALD. You know Ade.

LOUIS. That's precisely it. I didn't know Ade. And what's more, neither do you.

GERALD. Don't be unfair to her.

LOUIS. All our psychology has gone out of the window.

GERALD. Calm down. Remember the promise we made? "Women will never come between us, not even our wives." It holds good for you as well as me.

LOUIS. Yes. One Christmas evening, near the Belfort Lion. We were both in our teens.

GERALD. In remembrance of that great evening of friendship and of today's meeting, we'll install a little Belfort Lion here. Let's find a place.

LOUIS. Poor Gerald.

GERALD. Words are never important. It's actions that count. And Ade is incapable of a mean trick towards you. I'll call her and give her a good scolding. (*calls into the garden*) Ade. Ade.

136

LOUIS. Ade is not in the garden.

GERALD. Where is she?

LOUIS. I don't know.

GERALD. But you know she isn't in the garden?

LOUIS. Yes.

GERALD. What on earth went on between you two that was so important?

LOUIS. Nothing. Nothing. You remember she wanted a serious talk with me even before I told you about Helen.

GERALD. Why yes, that's right. What was this decisive conversation?

LOUIS. Well, it's like this . . . she asked me to tell you . . . Oh, it was quite an announcement.

GERALD. Now what mischief has Ade been up to?

LOUIS. How can I explain . . .

GERALD. Something serious?

LOUIS. Yes, very serious.

GERALD. She's stolen something from a department store? Signed a check in my name?

LOUIS. If only she had. And to think she might have been reproached for so little. No, it's much more serious than that.

GERALD. Where is she? Where has she gone?

LOUIS. I don't know.

GERALD. You do know.

LOUIS. I know and I don't know.

GERALD. Do I have to drag it out of you? Is it some trouble of a sentimental nature?

LOUIS. Yes.

GERALD. That's ridiculous.

LOUIS. That's what I told her.

GERALD. What caused her to become jealous all of a sudden?

LOUIS. Jealous of what?

GERALD. That's what I'd like to know. I've never deceived Ade, never even wanted to. Ade knows I adore her . . . I try to hide it as much as possible because she gets so excited. (*Bell rings. He jumps up.*) What's that?

LOUIS. It's Joseph ringing for the end of our recreation.

137

GERALD. Oh, of course.

LOUIS. Yes, it's right on seven o'clock.

GERALD. Where is Ade?

LOUIS. I'll try and explain. (*knock at trapdoor*)

GERALD. There she is. She's just been walking round the garden. Just another of her jokes, old man. That's her. But I certainly was getting worried. (*opening trapdoor*) Come up, you idiot, come up.

(*Enter Helen Donaldo.*)

HELEN. I counted the minutes, then the seconds. I waited for the bell. May I enter now?

GERALD. Who are you? What do you want?

LOUIS. Gerald, it's Helen. Don't you recognize her?

GERALD. I ask you for the last time, where is Ade?

HELEN. Ade? Isn't she here? Joseph told me she was with you.

GERALD. You know he's called Joseph and she's called Ade? Well!

HELEN. (*slightly disconcerted*) You are Gerald?

GERALD. Yes I am, and perhaps you can also tell me where my wife has run off to?

LOUIS. It's nothing, darling. I'll explain everything.

GERALD. It's nothing to you; and you'll explain everything to her . . .

HELEN. Yes. Tell me, Louis. I was so happy.

GERALD. (*having looked at them a moment*) Ade's gone to meet another man, hasn't she?

LOUIS. How can I tell you . . . wait, Helen . . . (*moves Helen gently away*)

GERALD. Who? Where?

LOUIS. I don't know.

GERALD. But you don't tell me I'm wrong, do you? I'm not deceiving myself, I'm being deceived. She's throwing herself into the arms of another man, as this woman throws herself into yours.

LOUIS. I said everything I could to prevent her leaving. I begged Ade . . .

GERALD. Yes, while you looked at your watch and waited for this little beauty, this fine example.

138

LOUIS. (*with Helen in his arms*) Forgive him, Helen. He's over-wrought.

GERALD. (*with photo*) My little Ade. My poor little girl. Get out of here, the pair of you. No. Wait. Before you go, tell me Mrs. Donaldo, did you not feel like going back, on your way over here, like returning to your husband?

HELEN. No.

GERALD. Then there is no hope of her coming back tonight?

HELEN. I love Louis more than anything else in the world.

GERALD. It's not true.

HELEN. You don't believe me?

GERALD. For God's sake don't tell me the very words she is saying to another man.

CURTAIN

ACT II

Three weeks later. A suite in a luxury hotel. At the back is a large terrace opening onto the sea and blue sky. A door at right leads to rooms occupied by Louis and Helen; a door at left leads to Gerald's room. Another door leads off to the corridor. It is 11:00 A.M. At the curtain's rise, we see Nicole, Helen, and Gerald.

NICOLE. When you left my hotel last night, did you walk back here as you planned?

GERALD. Yes. It was a beautiful night for a stroll.

HELEN. We were so happy.

NICOLE. (*emphasizing the word*) Happy?

139

GERALD. Happy to be walking under a myriad of stars. Happy for such peace. Helen, I'll see if I can shake Louis out of bed. (*exits*)

NICOLE. What a charming man.

HELEN. No one will ever know what he went through after his wife left him. It was terrible. Louis arranged this trip to try and take his mind off it, to help him forget his bitter memories.

NICOLE. What a charming man.

HELEN. Charming, yes, but sometimes hateful. Charming because that's his nature and hateful when he remembers the past.

NICOLE. Does he often think about it?

HELEN. Continually, until last night when he met you at dinner. You completely bowled him over.

NICOLE. Do you think I'll be able to console him?

HELEN. You may be hurt if his wife returns before the end of the treatment.

NICOLE. I like being hurt.

HELEN. Come now!

NICOLE. Helen, I'm just crazy about Gerald.

HELEN. Already?

NICOLE. You know how spontaneous I am! And Gerald is so melancholy. But last night, he took me into his confidence.

HELEN. And it must be so pleasant to repair someone else's damage; the same damage we ourselves have done to others; and be able to see our own handiwork at such close quarters.

NICOLE. But you don't understand. A man in his condition doesn't think about golf or politics or business. He's completely enamored with love. And I do enjoy it. Are you happy?

HELEN. Yes.

NICOLE. You love Louis very much?

HELEN. Even more than that.

NICOLE. Madly?

HELEN. No. Very calmly. (*pause*) It's a feeling I've never known before, I can't describe it. We change so completely, yet we only have the same words to explain ourselves as before. We used words without actually knowing their true meaning.

140

NICOLE. (*not understanding*) Really?

HELEN. He's the dearest man in the whole world. For me, there'll never be anyone else.

NICOLE. I understand you perfectly. It's a wonderful feeling. I've had it three or four times already . . .

HELEN. Yes, but it's the first time for me, and I'll always love Louis.

NICOLE. You don't really think Louis will be your last man, do you? Wait till the novelty has worn off. I mean at your age . . .

HELEN. I'm sure of it.

NICOLE. Even if you went on your own to the winter sports for a couple of weeks?

HELEN. Even if I had to live away from him for a whole year.

(*Gerald enters.*)

GERALD. Helen, go and see to Louis. I give up. He's so full of the joys of spring, I can't get a word in edgeways. He's looking all over the place for his tie. In the cupboards, under the bed . . .

HELEN. His tie?

GERALD. You know where it is?

HELEN. What a child. He doesn't need a tie. (*exits quickly, calling*) Louis!

NICOLE. They're so happy. (*Gerald groans.*) Stop groaning. Some day you'll be just as happy as they are.

GERALD. God forbid!

NICOLE. Don't you envy them?

GERALD. I feel sorry for them.

NICOLE. Sorry?

GERALD. I pity them. Look how they live. They don't know it yet, but they're living on credit. They'll have to pay for it some day. The day of reckoning always comes. Then they'll find out they're bankrupt.

NICOLE. You were so gay last night at the flower gala.

GERALD. Oh, I'm not sad. I've simply discovered, like millions of other people since the beginning of time, that life holds more misery than happiness. Here on earth, Hell is much more perfected than Heaven. Heaven must be run down here by a few respectable

141

old ladies and Hell by vigorous young people, full of action and spirit.

NICOLE. All these big words — Heaven, happiness, and Hell — they're all women, I suppose.

GERALD. No. (*pause*) Only one woman.

NICOLE. No one has the right to make a man like you suffer. That's what I think.

GERALD. Perhaps she doesn't know I'm suffering.

NICOLE. Gerald, I'd like so much to be your friend.

GERALD. You are my friend, Nicole.

NICOLE. Have you many women friends?

GERALD. Ever since I was first in love, I could never accept the idea that a woman could be a friend. It seemed to me that for a man, friendship meant another man. I had a friend once.

NICOLE. Isn't Louis still your friend?

GERALD. (*without conviction*) Yes . . .

NICOLE. (*surprised*) But I thought . . .

GERALD. (*meaningfully*) He's my best friend.

NICOLE. (*enthusiastically*) And Helen is so nice.

GERALD. Very nice. She came in one door as Ade walked out the other. (*dismally*) What a laugh!

NICOLE. Now, tell me something about your work.

GERALD. My work? Oh yes. I'll get back to it in Paris one of these days, I suppose. At the moment it's as enticing as a sink of dirty dishes.

NICOLE. Nonsense. Let me give you some friendly advice. When you return to Paris, keep on fighting, striving . . . I mean I want you to reach the top . . .

GERALD. What a romantic view of business.

NICOLE. Oh?

GERALD. Like my romantic view of love. Do you often tell lies?

NICOLE. Who to? My mother? Or the priest?

GERALD. She lied dreadfully to me. Yet I can't be sure. Did she lie to me? Maybe that's the very reason she left, so as not to lie.

NICOLE. What do you want me to say about her? Something good or something bad?

142

GERALD. Do you enjoy playing nurse to me?

NICOLE. I'm protecting my happiness.

GERALD. What do you mean?

NICOLE. Just that. No more, no less.

GERALD. Look at me, Nicole.

NICOLE. I love you, Gerald. You've swept me off my feet. All I can think of is you — and I must be mad to tell you.

GERALD. Oh no.

NICOLE. I feel so ashamed throwing myself at you like this.

GERALD. No, please.

NICOLE. But I'm prepared to suffer.

GERALD. Are you suffering?

NICOLE. Because I love you. (*They kiss.*) Hold me in your arms again. Hold me. I already loved you last night. Didn't you realize?

GERALD. No.

NICOLE. Gerald, I should be so proud to comfort you.

GERALD. I've been almost out of my mind for weeks. Imagine, not a word from her, not a word. I don't know where she is, who she's with, nothing.

NICOLE. You'll forget her eventually.

GERALD. I'm sure I shall.

NICOLE. And it'll happen all of a sudden, you'll see. Forgetting is as strange, as rapid, and as violent as loving. You know what it's like to be love-struck. Well, there's such a thing as being wind-struck.

GERALD. Wind-struck? Oh, I see. A great gust of wind sweeping everything away.

NICOLE. Take my word for it. Since my divorce . . .

GERALD. You are divorced?

NICOLE. Gerald, tell me we are going to be happy.

GERALD. Why not?

NICOLE. If only I'd known that one day I should meet you!

GERALD. What would you have done?

NICOLE. Waited for you.

GERALD. So now you have met me, you are even sorry for having loved your husband? Is that it?

NICOLE. (*stupidly*) Oh yes, but I also will be able to forget . . .

GERALD. The gust of wind . . . yes.

NICOLE. We're eating together at twelve, all four of us.

GERALD. All together. An excellent idea.

NICOLE. I know a quaint little restaurant by the shore where during Lent they serve a delicious teal dish, with lemon. Would you like that?

GERALD. Of course, why not?

NICOLE. Don't sound so enthusiastic!

GERALD. I was thinking about something else.

NICOLE. May I ask?

GERALD. What you said about the gust of wind.

NICOLE. You don't expect it to happen? Neither did I. Happiness creeps up on people.

GERALD. Maybe she was picked up by someone, too, and was as confused as you are.

NICOLE. Yes.

GERALD. And maybe he took her in his arms as I take you, and kissed her as I kiss you. (*pushes her away*)

NICOLE. Gerald?

GERALD. It's too painful.

NICOLE. Why?

GERALD. Don't you see? I feel as if I'm the other fellow.

NICOLE. What fellow?

GERALD. The one who held Ade in his arms like that. When I look into your eyes, all I can see is Ade's joy at deceiving me for the first time. When I'm with you, I can think only of her, nothing else. I only deceive myself as I play the other man's part.

NICOLE. You're being ridiculous.

GERALD. Perhaps. But if you are my friend, Nicole, go away. Please, go away.

NICOLE. But why?

GERALD. Because you are making me ill. When I look at you, all I see is her.

144

NICOLE. Are you going to fret over this woman all your life?

GERALD. I fret for my own happiness, not for her.

NICOLE. Ha! Where's the happiness in being a cuckold?

GERALD. I mean the happiness I knew when I loved her and thought she loved me.

NICOLE. You loved a ghost.

GERALD. Grieved as I am, I still feel like shouting, "Give me back my ghost." When you've known real suffering, even false happiness seems sweet.

NICOLE. (*despisingly*) I pity you, my friend.

GERALD. It doesn't sound very heroic, I know, but what do you offer for my comfort except the sight of a woman eager to give herself? Do you think I lacked imagination? Do you think I needed your demonstrations, your complicity, to know how Ade reacted in someone else's arms?

(*Enter Louis and Helen.*)

LOUIS. What's the matter now?

GERALD. I needed comfort and like a fool I let her make up to me.

NICOLE. I didn't make up to you.

GERALD. And the whole thing backfired.

NICOLE. Your friend is raving.

GERALD. Only a faithful woman can comfort me now, don't you realize that? To see a woman refusing herself, if there are any left. Go and enjoy your lunch. I'm not hungry anymore.

NICOLE. Your grief has made you coarse and vulgar, my friend. Goodbye. (*exits*)

GERALD. I'm sorry. I suffer as best I can, and I'll cure myself in my own way. (*pause*) But how? There are no virtuous women left.

LOUIS. Well now . . . er . . . I think if we found something else to talk about it would be much more sensible.

GERALD. Yes. I agree.

LOUIS. Sunbathing at half past eleven, all right? What better than a relaxing sunbath.

HELEN. Then into the water. I want to swim to the lighthouse before lunch.

(*There is a silence.*)

145

LOUIS. What do you say, old man?

GERALD. The water is too cold.

LOUIS. (*to Helen*) As I was saying, we'll sunbathe.

HELEN. So, two sunbaths for the gentlemen. Then we'll all come back and have lunch on this lovely terrace.

GERALD. Why play with words, Helen? There's absolutely nothing lovely about this terrace.

HELEN. Are you unfair even towards the countryside?

GERALD. This "lovely" terrace separates two rooms: yours, which is also Louis', and mine where I am alone. And oh God, this sun, and this relaxing sky. It all looks so happy, I can hardly bear it. If only it would rain!

LOUIS. And I told Helen you were an uncomplicated person.

GERALD. Maybe you also told her I was happy.

LOUIS. Pretend to be happy and you'll soon feel happy. Look, try and force yourself to sing all the time. It's one of Pascal's tricks. (*sings*)

> Listen! Listen! everything is fair,
> Listen! Listen! music fills the air!

GERALD. I want next year to come quickly for many reasons. But the main reason is to hear new songs which have no memories for me. Now I know why songs on the hit parade last such a short time, why everyone wants to forget so quickly the tunes they enjoyed singing so much before. It's because they want to forget all the stupid little things they associate them with . . .

HELEN. Why must you be so obstinately sentimental?

GERALD. Doesn't your ex-husband have songs to recall some happy evening he spent with you? Some joyous moment when the orchestra started to play a new tune? Perhaps he wishes they would change their repertoire, too.

HELEN. No, Gerald. My husband hasn't any songs. (*pause*)

GERALD. Not even a wedding march? (*exits*)

HELEN. I'd be the first to admit the cure's not doing him much good.

LOUIS. Let's pack our bags right away. I've had enough.

HELEN. No, Louis. We are the happy ones, it's up to us to be patient.

LOUIS. We won't see him again before we leave.

HELEN. No, Louis. Our happiness depends a little on his. We both know that. What we have to do is cure him.

LOUIS. He doesn't want to be cured.

HELEN. That's just a characteristic of his sickness. You want to leave. But when once you start thinking of how you left him . . . remember how you spent our first night of real freedom trying to comfort him?

LOUIS. A promising start, I must say. We've never had so little peace since we've been together. Your husband was much less of a nuisance.

HELEN. Don't be silly. I'm worried, Louis.

LOUIS. What about?

HELEN. Soon, you'll love me just a little less.

LOUIS. Nonsense.

HELEN. I'm becoming very solemn. I'm afraid to laugh in front of Gerald, and I'll end by irritating you. I'd like to dance and sing. You know how horribly selfish I am. I have to force myself to be interested in other people. I'm even a little indifferent to Gerald. Look at the sun. I'm crazy about the sun. I adore the sun — but only because it looks so well on you. You look so handsome in the sunlight.

LOUIS. (to sun) Thanks, sun!

HELEN. When it stops shining on you, I don't think about it any more. It might as well not be there. Just look at this table! It's terrible! Look at it. (laughs) It's awful. But you know, it really means something to me. The day we arrived, you put your hat on it, then both hands, like that, and you said, "Helen, how wonderful! We're going to be very happy here."

LOUIS. A touching quotation! But not exactly a scintillating picture of my present state of mind.

HELEN. Sit down and stop making fun of me. There. (sitting on his knees) You remember Pyla?

LOUIS. Yes.

HELEN. The day we got lost in the dunes?

LOUIS. Yes, I wasn't very proud of myself.

HELEN. That's not all. You don't know how close you came to disaster.

LOUIS. All right. Out with it. What's the big secret?

HELEN. A woman always has her secret. Here's mine about Pyla. When I saw how worried you were, completely lost, running all over the place trying to find the way, I had the wicked idea of hiding myself. You know, burying myself completely in the sand with a little straw in my mouth to breathe through, to make you feel I'd disappeared, vanished into thin air, been snuffed out by the breeze.

LOUIS. Very ingenious! I'd have spent hours searching for you. What held you back?

HELEN. With my ears full of sand, how could I have heard your pitiful little cries? (*sings*)

> I have lost my Eurydice,
> Nothing equals my distress . . .

LOUIS. You have mad ideas. But you're right. I should have invented the most heartrending cries to bring you back to me again.

HELEN. Darling. You see, even when Gerald's not here, our happiness is still sad.

LOUIS. Happiness is never sad or gay. It's just happiness.

HELEN. And I'm so happy. Only, we must find something to keep Gerald busy.

LOUIS. Yes. Introducing him to Nicole was a slight flop.

HELEN. Yet she's a lovely girl. You don't think too badly of me, Louis, do you?

LOUIS. Acting as a . . . what's the name . . . a go-between?

HELEN. I thought so. You do think badly of me.

LOUIS. You lack practice, that's all.

HELEN. If you knew how much I'd put into it. I was certain it would turn out all right. I could already hear myself telling Gerald not to thank me as my only thought was for your peace of mind.

148

LOUIS. When you're not thinking about me, who do you think about?

HELEN. Us.

LOUIS. I love you, Helen.

(*Gerald enters, wishing to appear calm.*)

GERALD. Am I disturbing you?

LOUIS. (*releasing himself*) No. Not in the least.

GERALD. I've been a fool, a complete fool. You're right, it is a lovely day. The sunshine is wonderful. I'm just a miserable devil, Louis. (*to Helen*) Please forgive me.

HELEN. There's nothing to forgive. We're friends.

GERALD. And Nicole, I was nauseating towards her, too. Do you think she'll forget about it?

HELEN. Perhaps.

GERALD. Didn't she upbraid me for using foul language or something?

LOUIS. Women of the world aren't afraid of a little foul language. Especially when it has a certain distinction.

GERALD. (*to Helen*) Tell me about Nicole. Was she very upset when her husband . . . I mean . . . when they separated?

HELEN. Poor girl. She's so captivating. And she's completely bowled over by you. Quite overwhelmed.

GERALD. So that's why she wanted me to have teal and lemon. Out of shyness, not stupidity.

LOUIS. Have you anything against eating teal in Lent?

GERALD. Using Lent as an excuse to create some fantastic new dish! Ha! And we all kid ourselves we're fasting when we've never eaten so well in our lives. How hypocritical!

HELEN. Don't be absurd. I know that little bistro.

LOUIS. (*jealously*) How do you know about it?

HELEN. Nicole told me. They say, once you've eaten there, you'll never forget it. If you promise to behave yourself, I'll phone Nicole. She'll forgive you. She has a heart of gold.

GERALD. Has it served her well since her divorce?

HELEN. She's a respectable woman.

GERALD. Has she had any lovers since then?

149

HELEN. (*with a vague gesture*) Divorced when she was nineteen, three or four years ago . . .

GERALD. One, two, three lovers?

HELEN. How should I know?

GERALD. How discreet! And she is a respectable woman. What does that mean nowadays? Our indulgence is becoming disconcerting. Thirty years ago, a divorced woman, no matter how respectable, was somebody of doubtful reputation and a little scandalous.

LOUIS. (*calmly, with false kindness*) How clear-sighted . . .

GERALD. I have my own ideas on what constitutes a respectable woman.

LOUIS. So have I.

HELEN. Fine. Let's go and sunbathe.

LOUIS. It's a woman in love.

GERALD. No.

LOUIS. (*provokingly*) No?

GERALD. No. A respectable woman is one who doesn't have two lovers at the same time.

LOUIS. (*taken aback*) That's the bare minimum.

GERALD. (*Helen having given up all attempts to stop them*) A respectable woman is one who doesn't let her husband think she loves him while making love to someone else. A respectable woman doesn't undress twice a day, first in a bachelor apartment, then at home with her husband when she goes to bed at night. A respectable woman doesn't use two bathrooms . . .

LOUIS. For God's sake have you no shame, you evil-minded blackguard?

HELEN. Louis!

LOUIS. Blackguard!

GERALD. You're right. But don't let us come to blows. Just leave me alone. I'm exhausted. Forgive me, Louis, but I know I'll just start all over again. We vowed once that women would never come between us. Well, you see, old friend, it's happened. They have destroyed our friendship by their devious methods.

LOUIS. You are drowning in your own tears. If you could only see yourself as I do.

150

GERALD. Wait till it's your turn, then we'll talk again.

LOUIS. My turn? (*to Helen*) Now he's insulting you.

GERALD. Is it an insult to think she could start all over again with somebody else, telling him the same lies you enjoyed so much?

LOUIS. You are mad.

GERALD. And wouldn't her actions be moral or immoral depending on whether you were the loved one or the victim?

HELEN. Please be quiet, the pair of you.

GERALD. Very well, let's say no more. Neither of you can help me. And I'll just poison your relationship if I haven't already done so. I'm leaving here . . . and later on . . .

LOUIS. Goodbye, Gerald.

GERALD. Let's take a last good look at each other, Louis.

LOUIS. Is it Helen's fault if Ade acted like a bitch?

GERALD. I hold nothing against Ade. I know nothing about her and I feel much tenderness towards her. But I detest you, Helen. I despise you. You are my misery, because you are the unfaithful woman.

HELEN. Leave me alone with Gerald.

LOUIS. No. Get your bags ready. I'll go to the garage.

GERALD. Don't go like this, Louis. Let's hope we will meet again someday.

LOUIS. I don't think so.

GERALD. Friends as we were?

LOUIS. I no longer have any friendship for you, Gerald. It's finished.

HELEN. I beg of you. Don't start again, please.

GERALD. (*to Helen*) I won't ask your forgiveness.

HELEN. It's I who ask for yours.

LOUIS. Why?

HELEN. I should have told you about Ade. I only kept quiet to help you forget her.

GERALD. But I don't want to forget Ade. Such an idea is intolerable to me.

LOUIS. What a spineless individual you are!

GERALD. If I thought I could forget her, I'd have to accept that she

151

could forget me. And I don't want her to forget she once loved me. No gust of wind, please. Anything but that.

LOUIS. Gust of wind? What are you babbling about?

GERALD. (*to Helen*) You are responsible for Ade leaving me, don't you see?

LOUIS. That's not true.

GERALD. (*to Louis*) If you hadn't been waiting for Helen that evening, you would have hung on to Ade, you would have held her back and not let her run away. You'd have told me what was happening and she'd still be with me now.

LOUIS. Helen, I want to be away before twelve.

GERALD. One more thing. That man she was meeting, was he already her lover?

LOUIS. I know nothing about it.

GERALD. Her first lover?

HELEN. I don't want to say anything bad about Ade. To judge a woman, one should know everything about her, and then some more. Let God who made us as we are do the judging — or judge himself for his handiwork. But if you want to go on living and keep sane, I advise you for your own sake . . .

GERALD. After you'd made love with Louis the first time — because there's always a first time — and you went home and saw your husband, he too, in a sense, for the first time . . .

LOUIS. Be careful, Gerald.

GERALD. Didn't you feel uneasy, embarrassed? No, you were happy and gay, weren't you? And your husband was perfectly happy to see you so happy. That's right, isn't it? He shared the happiness the other man had given you . . .

LOUIS. Helen, if you don't leave with me this minute, I promise you, I'll let him have it!

(*The door opens and Achilles enters.*)

ACHILLES. (*very timid*) I'm sorry, but I knocked four times counting five between each knock and knocking louder and louder every time.

HELEN. What do you want?

ACHILLES. I wish to speak to Mr. Gerald Barbier.

152

GERALD. That's me.

ACHILLES. I know. I know you.

GERALD. Well, you've picked the wrong day, do you hear? Come back some other time. Louis . . .

ACHILLES. I've come on behalf of your wife.

GERALD. What?

ACHILLES. Allow me to introduce myself. I am Achilles Bellorson.

GERALD. (*who hasn't listened*) On behalf of my wife?

ACHILLES. Yes, sir.

GERALD. (*shaking*) Who the devil are you?

ACHILLES. I repeat, I am Mr. Achilles Bellorson.

GERALD. What in God's name is that supposed to tell me. I'm asking you . . .

HELEN. Mr. Barbier is asking you in what capacity you are here.

ACHILLES. His wife has given me a message for him.

GERALD. My wife. You know my wife?

ACHILLES. Yes.

GERALD. Since when?

ACHILLES. Well, er . . .

GERALD. Where is she?

ACHILLES. I er . . .

GERALD. When did you see her last?

ACHILLES. Ten minutes ago.

LOUIS. Then she is here?

ACHILLES. In the hotel? Oh no, I swear she isn't.

GERALD. But who are you?

ACHILLES. I've told you, I am . . .

GERALD. You are not her lover, surely?

ACHILLES. May I point out very calmly that I have come here to speak, not to listen.

GERALD. Speak.

ACHILLES. It's like this . . .

GERALD. Out with it . . . this errand boy! Her lover!

ACHILLES. I never said anything of the sort.

GERALD. Then who are you?

ACHILLES. Achilles Bellorson. And I am here because Ade . . .

153

GERALD. Ade! Ade! Can't you say Mrs. Barbier?

ACHILLES. I don't mind, but it wouldn't change matters in the slightest.

HELEN. Calm down, Gerald, and let him speak.

GERALD. (to Louis) Do you know him?

LOUIS. No.

GERALD. Did Ade ever mention him to you?

LOUIS. Never.

GERALD. What is your name?

ACHILLES. Achilles Bellorson.

GERALD. I know that, man, I know that. Go on. Go on.

ACHILLES. Three weeks ago, your wife left home . . .

GERALD. (bursting) And you came to tell me that?

ACHILLES. I was beginning a long-prepared speech. Had I not been ordered to come here, I'd much rather have been elsewhere, believe me.

GERALD. With Ade, perhaps?

ACHILLES. Oh, I don't know.

GERALD. What do you mean?

HELEN. Sit down, Gerald.

GERALD. Well sir, I'm listening.

ACHILLES. Try, at least. It's like this. Ade . . . I mean your wife . . . your ex-wife . . .

GERALD. My ex-wife!

LOUIS. What is this all about?

ACHILLES. You are Louis, aren't you?

GERALD. Oh, wonderful! He knows your name, too.

ACHILLES. (to Louis) Ade would like him to forgive her.

GERALD. For what?

HELEN. Don't be difficult, Gerald. For leaving you, obviously.

GERALD. First of all, how long have you known my wife? And why did she pick you to bring this message?

ACHILLES. She has ordered me not to give any solution to the hypotheses you might formulate!

GERALD. Take me to her.

ACHILLES. I don't have the right.

154

LOUIS. Why does she want his forgiveness?

ACHILLES. (*to Gerald*) Since she went away, she's been most concerned about you; about how grief-stricken you must be. She waited anxiously for news of your suicide . . .

GERALD. Really!

ACHILLES. You know what she's like . . .

GERALD. Oh yes. (*suddenly, in another tone*) And you?

ACHILLES. She simply instructed me to bring back your forgiveness.

GERALD. If she was so concerned about me, why didn't she ever send me any news?

ACHILLES. She never wrote to you?

GERALD. Not a word. What's so funny?

ACHILLES. My position is horribly embarrassing, you understand. Ade told me she hadn't written to you . . .

HELEN. Will you be seeing Mrs. Barbier again this morning?

ACHILLES. Yes, if she hasn't changed her mind.

HELEN. And she's longing for Gerald to forgive her?

ACHILLES. Yes.

HELEN. Tell her she's forgiven.

GERALD. And that she is to come back immediately.

ACHILLES. Come back? She never said anything about coming back. Now she's forgiven, she won't be anxious about you anymore, that's all. (*to Louis*) You've no idea what she's been through, worrying about Ger . . . Mr. Barbier.

GERALD. (*bursting*) He was going to say "Gerald."

ACHILLES. I'm sorry. You may not know it, but you're one of the important characters in my life.

GERALD. Come along with me, then. Or rather, I'll follow you. Take me to her.

ACHILLES. No, sir, I can't.

LOUIS. Where is she staying?

ACHILLES. I can't tell you.

GERALD. Do you think I'm going to let you slip away just like that?

ACHILLES. Ade lent me her revolver. (*showing it*) I promise you, in my present state, I'd shoot you without even realizing what I was doing. I know it would be criminal, but I am no longer in

155

any condition not to shoot if you follow me. I am further distressed to see you all so worked up like this. If only you knew how desperately I needed a little calm.

LOUIS. Well, I'm calm. As Mrs. Barbier seems to have taken you into her confidence, you must know she has complete confidence in me. I'll go with you, then Ade will be able . . .

ACHILLES. No sir. Ade is in hiding and wishes to remain so.

GERALD. (*to Louis*) Are you going to be influenced by . . .

ACHILLES. I'm quite a reasonable person, normally. But I gave Ade my word, and if you try to follow me, I shall have to shoot you. (*to Gerald*) You can be sure I'll tell your wife everything exactly as it happened. I don't have the strength to lie anymore.

GERALD. Will it be soon?

ACHILLES. If she waited where I left her, she'll know in five minutes.

GERALD. And tell her I insist she come back immediately.

ACHILLES. Goodbye, sir. My apologies. (*exits*)

GERALD. (*to Louis*) Did Ade give you any hint of such a weird individual before she left?

LOUIS. Not exactly.

GERALD. It can't be him, surely?

HELEN. As you said yourself, is there another man in the first place?

GERALD. I'm just amazed.

HELEN. One thing is certain. Your wife is close at hand and longs to see you.

GERALD. Unless that crazy halfwit is also a practical joker. We didn't ask for any proof. We should have asked him if Ade is a blonde or a brunette.

HELEN. What will you think of next?

GERALD. Perhaps she's dyed her hair.

LOUIS. He knew our Christian names, remember.

GERALD. So does the postman.

LOUIS. But this message and this young man, isn't it all typical of Ade?

HELEN. You'll be hearing from your wife inside five minutes.

GERALD. You really think so?

HELEN. I'm positive.

156

LOUIS. An absolute certainty!

GERALD. What shall I do?

HELEN. Be calm, listen to her, and believe all she says.

GERALD. Why? Do you think she is going to lie?

HELEN. No. But she'll be a little afraid to begin with.

GERALD. If she comes.

HELEN. She already knows you forgive her. (*telephone rings*)

LOUIS. There she is.

HELEN. No, wait. Let me answer it. (*taking receiver*) Yes . . . yes . . . a person in the foyer asking for Mr. Gerald Barbier . . . on behalf of Mrs. Ade Barbier.

GERALD. Tell her to come up! Straight away! Tell her to come up.

HELEN. Please show this person to the apartment. Thank you. (*replaces receiver*)

LOUIS. She was obviously waiting in the lobby.

GERALD. How shall I greet her? Forgive me, Helen, for all the stupid things I've said. I want to kiss you like a grateful brother.

HELEN. Calm down, first.

GERALD. (*to Louis*) Don't you see? When I seemed angry with you, it was only my grief speaking to me, that's all.

HELEN. If Ade's departure was ill-timed, we must admit the timing of her return couldn't be better.

LOUIS. You know Ade's flare for the dramatic. Sending that young boy with a revolver. If you let that pass, you'll never hear the end of it. I have an idea.

GERALD. What is it? Quickly.

LOUIS. Let us all behave as normal. Ade has never been away. All four of us have been here on holiday for a week now and the holiday continues. Nothing has happened. Everything is perfectly normal.

HELEN. Wonderful!

GERALD. It's fine with me.

LOUIS. As if nothing had happened.

GERALD. But you'd better telephone to cancel the teal dinner.

LOUIS. Don't start complicating things already.

157

HELEN. I'll come back here in ten minutes in my bathing suit. And I'll shout, "Ade, Ade, how are you this morning?"

LOUIS. "Now to the beach, everybody."

GERALD. But she hates bathing in the sea.

LOUIS. Nonsense. She's loved the beach for a week now.

GERALD. I'm telling you, she's afraid of the water. (*knock at the door*) Come in! Come in!

HELEN. Wait. Keep calm.

LOUIS. We'll be back in ten minutes.

HELEN. Call us, if necessary.

(*There is another knock. They both exit.*)

GERALD. Come in, darling, come in.

(*The door opens. A very serious-looking man is there.*)

JULES. Mr. Gerald Barbier?

GERALD. Yes . . . (*Jules wishes to enter.*) There must be some mistake.

JULES. No, I don't think so.

GERALD. (*exasperated*) I repeat, there must be some mistake. Be good enough to leave.

JULES. Are you expecting someone?

GERALD. Yes. But not you.

JULES. It is me, I'm afraid.

GERALD. No, I tell you. It's not you.

JULES. Then why did you tell the hall porter to show me up?

GERALD. I thought it was my wife . . .

JULES. It was me. But I do come on your wife's behalf.

GERALD. (*collapsing*) Ooooh!

JULES. I should perhaps add that by a strange coincidence, your wife isn't the only one who invited me here.

GERALD. Oh? Who else?

JULES. Yourself.

GERALD. Me?

JULES. Let me introduce myself. I am Jules Donaldo, Helen's husband. I understand she's your friend's mistress at the moment.

GERALD. You are Mr. Donaldo? Oh, I just don't know where I am anymore.

158

JULES. May I sit down?

GERALD. Where is my wife?

JULES. Like yourself, she's very disturbed.

GERALD. But the hall porter telephoned that my wife wanted to see me . . .

JULES. No, he said, "a person." He did ask me what name to give, and since my name might have triggered off a whole series of related dramas, and since I had come on your wife's behalf, I told the straightforward truth, "on behalf of Mrs. Barbier."

GERALD. Oh no. No. That would be the very end. You couldn't be my wife's lover?

JULES. No, Mr. Barbier. Your wife is charming, but I don't have a mistress. Though, I admit, it would have been pleasant to have run off with your wife on the very day your friend was running off with mine. But life doesn't have the dramatic refinements of your dear wife. I'm just a lonely man like yourself. I received your letter.

GERALD. (*embarrassed*) It was stupid, I know. Forgive me. I was in such a state when I wrote it . . . I didn't even read it over . . .

JULES. It touched me very much. And life is so exciting. Because your wife came to see me two days later.

GERALD. She came to see you?

JULES. Yes.

GERALD. What did she want?

JULES. I might ask you the same question.

GERALD. I thought about you very much and wondered how you were bearing your misfortune. I've borne mine very badly. I almost go mad sometimes. And one night when I really was mad, I felt you were the only person who could console me. So I wrote you that letter. You must have been surprised.

JULES. Yes. For a moment, I suspected it was some sort of joke in very bad taste. Then your wife came to see me.

GERALD. Where is she?

JULES. In town.

GERALD. Did you travel with her from Paris?

JULES. No. She told me to meet her here as soon as she heard where you were.

GERALD. She even knows where I'm staying?

JULES. I suspect she followed you last night to the casino. It appears you dined there with friends and an attractive young girl.

GERALD. What! She was there, spying on me, while I was trying to forget her with that girl?

JULES. Ade could be lying, but she swore she'd followed you and that you had dined at the casino. If you really went there, I suppose she could be telling the truth.

GERALD. But why did she write to you?

JULES. You wrote to me, didn't you?

GERALD. Who is her lover?

JULES. Ah! I don't know.

GERALD. Does she have one?

JULES. Why ask me? Don't you know?

GERALD. In Heaven's name, tell me all you can.

JULES. She came to see me three days ago in Paris, said she knew where Helen, my wife, was, and asked me to join her here. And as you yourself had asked to see me . . .

GERALD. I'm sorry I wrote to you.

JULES. Why?

GERALD. I was hoping your suffering would have calmed me, but you don't seem to be suffering at all.

JULES. Why should I?

GERALD. Don't you love your wife?

JULES. Have I ever suggested I didn't?

GERALD. Let's get this over with. Have you come to tell me why Ade sent that gun-waving adolescent here?

JULES. First I've heard of it.

GERALD. A quarter of an hour ago.

JULES. Your wife called me five minutes ago to say you'd forgiven her and were waiting for me.

GERALD. I wasn't waiting for you at all.

JULES. I have the feeling she likes dramatic situations.

GERALD. How could you accept such a vague assignment?

JULES. I find this all rather irritating. She wanted me to come. You wanted me to come. I forgot to mention I myself wanted to come . . . and you ask me what I am doing here!

GERALD. Yes, I do.

JULES. May I sit down? Thank you. Well, Mr. Barbier, I suppose you see quite a lot of Helen? (*Gerald indicates an indifferent "yes."*) Adorable, isn't she?

GERALD. Has Ade decided to come back to me?

JULES. My dear fellow, how young you are! Our wives always come back to us. A word of advice: When she does return, give her some children. Women would have fewer lovers if they had more children. I'm telling you this little trick of the trade because I like you. Now, tell me, is Helen happy?

GERALD. I don't know.

JULES. And your friend? They say he's quite a fine specimen.

GERALD. Correct me if I'm wrong, but your wife's little escapade doesn't seem to bother you. Would you regard her behavior as more or less normal?

JULES. Normal? I'm twenty years older than my wife, is that normal? Now if I were a romantic poet, a great explorer or somebody like that with fixed ideals, a hanger of dreams, a lighter of stars — but I'm a gravel merchant.

GERALD. And because you sell gravel, does that allow you to accept lies and betrayals?

JULES. You are using old words to judge a new situation. If such errors of judgment were made by boards of directors, they'd soon find themselves bankrupt. You talk of betrayal, but you can't betray something which no longer exists. The time has gone when the purpose of marriage was to start a family and a man married his wife forever. Today, my friend, religion means nothing to our wives. And whose fault is it? Do we go to church? No. And so the only morality left to them is "love," the most uncertain, most ill-defined word in the human vocabulary. In a single day, it can express a whole variety of conflicting sentiments. Have you ever tried explaining to your wife why she should always love you, and no one else?

161

GERALD. But look . . .

JULES. Why should she? Because it pleases you? How can you construct a whole philosophy of life on such petty selfishness?

GERALD. And you find comfort in such claptrap!

JULES. I do what I can.

GERALD. Didn't you try to find someone else, first?

JULES. At my age? Besides, she's irreplaceable.

GERALD. For you, perhaps.

JULES. If you only knew how she worshiped me, how she kept proving her love to me every day for two and a half years.

GERALD. When you were first married?

JULES. No. During the time it seems she was your friend's mistress.

GERALD. What?

JULES. Let me explain.

GERALD. Some other time. Consider for one minute and you'll realize how impossible it is for you to remain here.

JULES. Why?

GERALD. Because they'll be coming back.

JULES. I don't mind leaving but . . .

GERALD. But what?

JULES. I'm expecting your wife to phone me here. She wouldn't answer to anybody else.

GERALD. If Helen came in . . .

JULES. She knows me.

GERALD. What about Louis?

JULES. He's had two and a half years to get used to me, hasn't he?

GERALD. No. He's very jealous.

JULES. Really? Well, let me assure you, I don't have a revolver, and I'm always very correct in situations that aren't.

(*Enter Louis.*)

LOUIS. (*in bathing wrap*) Ade! Ade! Hello Ade!

GERALD. Where is Helen?

LOUIS. She'll be right down.

GERALD. Don't let her come down here.

LOUIS. Why?

162

JULES. A handsome fellow. Very likable. I can well understand Helen. I'm her husband.

LOUIS. You, Helen's husband? What are you doing here?

JULES. I had a message for Mr. Barbier. And I thought I might say hello to my wife at the same time . . . if that's all right with you . . . if not . . . I don't want to put you out in any way. No doubt you think I have some ulterior motive in coming here. But you know, when you've lived a little and acquired some common sense, you lose all desire for pettiness. And if you're not frightened by death as it approaches, you become aware of having grown in stature, of a certain dignity. Your horizons are extended, broadened. I'm sure you are familiar with the point of view of Sirius. Well, there is also the point of view of death. But I'm talking too much. (*pause*) Well, I'll be on my way. I have seen you and that is already a beginning.

(*Enter Helen in bathing suit.*)

HELEN. Down to the beach, everybody! (*Shocked, she drops her bathing hat. Feeling very uncomfortable in her attire, she puts her hat back on her head with difficulty, preferring not to move. Pause.*) What are you doing here?

JULES. And yourself?

HELEN. You know very well what I'm doing here. And if you've come just to hear it from me, I won't disappoint you. I'm with the man I love.

JULES. Why be aggressive? Because we loved each other and you went away? (*to Louis*) If you don't enjoy seeing me, remember I can also see you. And you are the less to be pitied . . . you have had two and a half years to become accustomed to me. Now, we face certain difficulties, to be sure. But am I responsible for them?

LOUIS. Who asked you to come?

JULES. Three different people — without any prompting from me.

GERALD. I should never have asked you to come here.

JULES. Even if I'd refused all news of your wife except in this lounge?

HELEN. (*to Gerald*) What's been going on?

LOUIS. (*to Gerald*) Was it you who . . .

JULES. I only came because his wife — Ade, I believe you call her — asked me to come. (*to Helen*) I rather think she saw you at the casino yesterday, introducing Mr. Barbier to an attractive young blonde.

LOUIS. Don't you think you ought to be leaving?

JULES. Haven't you anything more to say to me, Helen?

HELEN. No.

JULES. (*moving to exit*) Oh, while I think of it, the two little parakeets are dead.

HELEN. My two little parakeets?

JULES. Don't reproach yourself. I don't think they died of grief or negligence, because I really took great care of them. But perhaps I didn't go about it in the proper way, I don't know.

HELEN. Why didn't Josephine look after them as she always does?

JULES. The day after you . . . after I returned home, I gave Josephine a holiday. She hadn't seen her people for a long time. She's such a sweet girl. She wanted to stay and look after me because of . . . Oh, well, I must be going. It warms my heart to see you so happy. I mean it. (*to Louis*) You should thank me for not making a scene. I entirely approve of Helen . . . since she couldn't resist going away with you any longer. Your friend here told me he'd been very distressed, but you see how everything straightens itself out; his wife is coming back, he won't suffer any more, and all four of you will be perfectly happy. (*to Helen*) Don't worry about me. I'll look after myself much better than I looked after your parakeets.

HELEN. I'm sorry if I distressed you.

JULES. Why be sorry? You are not responsible for the thousand and one disorders of our time. I only reproach you for one thing.

HELEN. I know. I ought to have told you about all this in the beginning.

JULES. Not at all. You couldn't have given me a finer proof of your love.

LOUIS. What proof?

JULES. Don't you understand? It is quite clear.

164

GERALD. Are you sure my wife is going to call you here?

JULES. Quite sure. Don't be nervous. You'll be having lunch with her and your friends. I'm sorry I'm not invited. I'm so lonely these days, and it will be such a curious sort of meal. No, Helen, I only wish you had let me know you were going away. You'd have spared me so much worry.

HELEN. Worry? My note was clear enough.

JULES. Very clear. But I didn't find it that evening. You put it under my pajamas. I waited up for you, fully clothed . . . and almost went out of my mind. I imagined you'd fallen under a bus, or been abducted . . . by hoodlums. I roused the police commissioner out of bed in the middle of the night. And when he suggested you might be having a night on the tiles, I promptly dismissed the idea saying you'd have told me. He said in such cases it wasn't exactly customary! Why didn't you say anything to me? Were you afraid you wouldn't have the courage to leave if you saw me again?

HELEN. I'm very sorry.

LOUIS. Helen couldn't foresee that her note . . .

JULES. I toured the hospitals all night. It was frightful. Finally, at about twelve the next morning, Josephine fortunately came across your letter. It was wrong to go without telling me. I should have understood . . . we could have told our friends you'd gone to the winter sports, then to the spring skiing, and when you came back . . .

LOUIS. Came back?

HELEN. Jules, I have great friendship for you. I'm very fond of you. And I didn't want to be cruel, but you force me into it. I love Louis.

JULES. Since when?

HELEN. Since the day I met him.

JULES. Then you have indeed been very kind, both of you, to put up with me for two and a half years.

LOUIS. Yes, far too kind.

JULES. Oh, but don't feel too badly about it. Helen and I were friends, more than anything. Very old friends in a quiet sort of way. But I was less lonely with her sleeping beside me, and when she woke up at night . . .

LOUIS. She slept with you?

HELEN. Louis, I love you. Now not another word. And you, Jules, if you are still my friend . . .

LOUIS. Didn't you have two bedrooms?

JULES. Oh, there are plenty of bedrooms in the house.

HELEN. If you hurt Louis, I shall never forgive you.

JULES. What could he be thinking of? I was a very placid old husband. (*The two men look at each other.*)

HELEN. It's not true!

JULES. What isn't true? Very well, I was even less than placid.

LOUIS. You used to sleep in the same bed all the time?

JULES. No. Only at night. But then I couldn't be absolutely sure about that. Helen can give you all the details. I should never forgive myself if I upset you. Still, there are one or two small things . . . Since you came here on holiday, I have been reliving every day of these last two and a half years. And all of them have withered one after another like flowers touched by the devil.

HELEN. (*moving to leave*) Louis, if you intend listening to any more of this, I'll leave you to it.

LOUIS. Stay with me.

JULES. I'm just leaving, Helen. Don't be so impatient. You both have your lives before you. Oh, tell me something. Sometime last year, Helen suddenly complained of feeling very tired and went away for two weeks to Pyla. Did she go with you, perhaps?

LOUIS. Of course.

JULES. How lucky! I'm groping forward very cautiously, you see. She may well have hidden the real reason for her trip from you, too. Just think how disastrous that could be!

HELEN. What are you trying to insinuate with your malicious mind?

JULES. (*to Louis*) Was the trip a failure?

LOUIS. A failure?

JULES. I assumed it was, because she was never more loving toward me than when she came home from Pyla.

166

HELEN. He's lying to try and hurt you.

LOUIS. You told me going home was unbearable, and that you felt lonelier than ever.

JULES. Don't accuse her. The whole thing is quite clear. After the novelty wore off, she became bored with you and returned to her "old friend." Isn't that it?

HELEN. (to Jules) I'm no longer your friend.

JULES. Don't be so silly. Admit you were far happier coming back from Pyla than after your trip to Copenhagen.

LOUIS. Copenhagen?

JULES. Yes. Twelve days in Copenhagen . . . Oh, excuse me. I am stupid. You couldn't know about that, of course. It was more than three years ago. She went there on her own, too. How time flies!

HELEN. (to Jules) Have you no shame?

JULES. Oh, that look. (laughs) It reminds me of your story about Mégève. She was with you, I know that now. But do you know how I found out? Helen was brilliant.

LOUIS. (seeing Helen move) Stay, Helen.

JULES. The story's worth it. Theresa, one of her close friends, spotted you both in some nightclub while you were there and she was afraid tongues might start wagging. So when Helen came back, she said to me, "Just imagine, I met Theresa there; she was behaving terribly badly and flirting outrageously with some gigolo or other by the name of Louis Deshayes."

HELEN. I didn't say that.

JULES. You surprise me, because I have a good memory. You may not have thought it, but those were your words. Anyhow, she said, "Since I was rather bored, I had the mad idea of turning on the charm and taking Theresa's little partner away from her. I acted like a tart and Theresa was absolutely furious." Well, I, like a good husband, asked for some information about this poor fellow — that is to say, about you. And she said, "Oh, I don't know. He wasn't a bit interesting. Needless to say, I'm in Theresa's bad books and she is saying the most horrible things about me and this gigolo." I believed Helen, as you would have done, and I laughed at her clever prank. I must admit, I still laugh at it.

LOUIS. Have you finished now?

JULES. Yes. I don't want to impose on your time. I only had one more question to ask, but I won't bother, because I'm sure I must be mistaken.

LOUIS. What question?

JULES. (*to Helen*) When my father died two years ago, you pleaded some story about going to the dressmaker's so that you could leave the day after me. Was it to spend your first night together? (*Pause. Then to Louis*) I forgive you, you didn't know me. Perhaps you never had a father, and Helen didn't like mine. But on that first night, did she tell you I'd gone to bury my father?

LOUIS. Yes.

JULES. I was hoping I might have been wrong.

HELEN. I left you because the life of lying sickened me, and because I wanted to be his, and his alone, without having to lie. Now I know I've loved only one man in my life, and that's Louis.

JULES. I don't condemn you for lying. Your lies are precious to me, because you lied in order to keep me. What more could I ask! (*to Louis*) Even the first time, when you were quite novel and mysterious.

LOUIS. How modest you are!

HELEN. Gerald, for pity's sake, ask them to be quiet.

JULES. Am I so modest? Weren't you aware of your defeat the very first day? I would have thought it humiliating for such an attractive young man to see his mistress leave him for another man on their first night together.

LOUIS. So in your eyes, the lover is humiliated and the husband never more triumphant than when he greets his unfaithful wife? You are a poet, sir, and a damned funny one at that.

JULES. Maybe that's because you and I and those like us have bled love of its greatness. I'm sure you are well aware that my wife is a rich woman. I simply want to point out she is not dependent on me and never has been and in the last three weeks, she's proved as much. Now two and a half years ago, she met an

168

attractive young man, someone new, handsome, free. Yet despite this, she left her seducer every evening to come home and spend the night with me. Why did she come back if it wasn't me she preferred? Finally, one day, she didn't come back. But for two and a half years, I resisted your charm — a charm I didn't even know about. She learned the art of lying, sometimes in the face of great difficulties, all so as not to lose me, to keep me by her side. I was the one she preferred. (*to Gerald*) As I said to you: a magnificent proof of love. (*to Louis*) For two and a half years, your "great love" was no more than a joke.

HELEN. That's not true.

JULES. Whatever people may say, the cuckold is nearly always the lover. Think about it.

GERALD. And you find comfort in such paradoxes! How can you believe that?

JULES. Well, I don't have the feeling of being paradoxical when I look at your friend's face here.

LOUIS. You make me feel sick.

GERALD. (*to Jules*) I admit she lied to keep you, but she still lied.

JULES. Everyone lies, my friend, even I. I lied about your wife phoning me here.

GERALD. (*indignant*) And you let me go on hoping . . .

JULES. Don't worry. She is waiting outside in the hall. (*He goes out and returns immediately with Ade. She falls at Gerald's feet.*) Don't they make a delightful picture?

ADE. Gerald, my darling, let me look at you. It's really you. Forgive me. Please forgive me.

JULES. Your husband asked me what he must forgive you for. I haven't the vaguest idea and neither has he.

ADE. You know nothing about it?

GERALD. Tell me quickly. I want to know everything.

ADE. You know I went away.

GERALD. Who with?

ADE. Who with? Why does there have to be anyone else? I know how to get around by myself. (*looking at Helen*) Oh, I can guess who you are. (*to Jules*) Won't you introduce me to your wife?

169

LOUIS. Hello, Ade!

ADE. Hello, Louis. (*to Gerald*) Why are they both in bathing suits? Is it some sort of uniform?

JULES. Excuse me. I must be going.

ADE. Why leave us so soon?

JULES. As I said, I don't wish to be a nuisance. I prefer you all to be happy together.

ADE. Happy! Oh no. Not yet. First, you must give me time to console poor Gerald. Gerald, tell me how much you have suffered.

GERALD. My suffering is over.

ADE. Even before I've consoled you?

GERALD. Your presence is enough to console me.

JULES. (*to Louis*) My apologies. (*to Gerald*) My compliments. (*to Ade*) My respects. (*to Helen*) My best wishes for your happiness.

HELEN. Jules, I shall never never come back to you.

JULES. See you soon, Helen.

CURTAIN

ACT III

Two hours later. Suitcases and trunks are scattered about the stage. Ade, hidden from the audience, is sleeping on the couch. Gerald and Helen enter from the terrace.

GERALD. She's not here.

LOUIS. (*coming out of his room*) She's not in our room. Where has she gone, now?

HELEN. (*to Gerald*) In your room, perhaps.

170

GERALD. I'll have a look. (*exits*)

LOUIS. (*worried*) And yet she seemed calm enough during lunch.

HELEN. Quite calm.

LOUIS. Were you taken in by it?

HELEN. By what?

LOUIS. By everything she said.

HELEN. Were you?

GERALD. (*entering*) No!

HELEN. (*seeing Ade*) Oh, Gerald!

GERALD. What is it?

HELEN. Sssh!

LOUIS. She's asleep.

HELEN. (*taking hold of Louis*) Come on. Let's finish packing.

LOUIS. I've had the big trunk brought down here.

HELEN. Come and help me.

(*They exit. Gerald looks at Ade.*)

GERALD. My sweet little Ade.

ADE. (*waking*) Gerald, I had a terrible nightmare.

GERALD. There, there.

ADE. I dreamed you were far, far away. I was calling you and I couldn't even hear my own voice.

GERALD. Lie down and rest.

ADE. I fell asleep.

GERALD. Like a baby.

ADE. No, like Curly. I often told you about Curly, didn't I . . . my little dog. He was a present for my first communion, but he died.

GERALD. Ade, don't think about such sad things.

ADE. Once he ran away for four days. We thought he was lost and I cried my heart out. I spent hours at the dog pound. I filled the newspapers with advertisements. And then on the morning of the fourth day, back he came home again, and into my bedroom. I was asleep. He saw me but didn't bark or even yelp. He made a woof and went to sleep, for twelve whole hours. It was the emotion of coming home again. I slept just like he did. I thought

171

I was meant to live great dramas. Well, it's not true. The emotion of it all is too much for me.

GERALD. What emotion?

ADE. Coming home again.

GERALD. I keep telling you, you didn't go away. You've been here with us for a week now. And you love bathing in the sea. You never left me . . .

ADE. Oh no. I can't allow you to let me off scot-free like that.

GERALD. Don't spoil my happiness.

ADE. It's inconceivable. I go away on my own for three weeks . . .

GERALD. And since you were on your own . . .

ADE. I mean without you . . . I feel very sinful.

GERALD. No, you are not.

ADE. How do you know?

GERALD. This whole affair is meaningless. It never happened. You never left me.

ADE. So, for those three weeks you lived . . .

GERALD. In perfect calm.

ADE. With your dear friend, Louis.

GERALD. With my dear friend, Louis.

ADE. I can't bear all this pretense.

GERALD. I'm not pretending. I'm happy.

ADE. But that's not what I want.

GERALD. You don't want me to be happy?

ADE. First, I swear to you it's not true.

GERALD. What?

ADE. I kept asking myself what Curly could have been up to all those four nights he was away. And I was only a little girl then.

GERALD. But you never left me.

ADE. Oh, you are more infuriating now than in the garret.

GERALD. Did the garret upset you?

ADE. It seemed the brightest moment in your day was meeting Louis there. That was too much for any woman to bear. I try to explain how exasperating it was, and I find I can go off for three weeks without you even batting an eyelid. But Gerald, I wasn't alone those three weeks.

172

GERALD. You were with Achilles. You told me all about it. You explained the whole thing.

ADE. Did I? I don't know what I told you anymore. I tried to reassure you, that's all.

GERALD. Reassure me?

ADE. You spoke to me as if I'd just come from the hairdresser's. Yet I was away three weeks. You honestly believed my story?

GERALD. (*paling*) All right. Tell me the whole truth.

ADE. What truth?

GERALD. There's only one truth. What were you doing those three weeks?

ADE. Gerald, please!

GERALD. You had a lover!

ADE. Really!

GERALD. Yes or no?

ADE. And if it's yes?

GERALD. Achilles . . . He was just a screen for someone else, wasn't he? Who was it?

ADE. (*with disarming smile*) Achilles hid no one.

GERALD. Don't worry. I'll forgive you.

ADE. Why?

GERALD. Looking at you, I can't believe I was so unhappy.

ADE. And when you don't look at me?

GERALD. I was so calm, so peaceful.

ADE. While I was away?

GERALD. No. Since you've come back. Before that, if you only knew how . . .

ADE. Here's what I want to know. Did you think about me very much? You noticed I didn't write to you?

GERALD. Those three weeks, Ade, I hardly slept more than an hour at a time. At nine o'clock, I thought, "They're already in bed, in each other's arms."

ADE. Did you really?

GERALD. During the night, at two in the morning, I thought, "No. They've been out and they're just coming in now." Then, in the

173

morning . . . Oh, I didn't sleep a wink for three long weeks because I didn't let either of you sleep.

ADE. Darling! You have tears in your eyes.

GERALD. Why didn't you write to me?

ADE. It wouldn't have been leaving you if I'd written every day.

GERALD. I never knew there could be such agony.

ADE. The truth is you suffered, you love me, and I adore you. We've never loved each other so much as now.

GERALD. Oh, my darling!

(*Enter Louis and Helen.*)

LOUIS. Are we disturbing you? It's just my shirts and underpants.

HELEN. We're nearly finished.

ADE. What? Are you really leaving? But this hotel is delightful, the town is so quaint.

HELEN. (*indifferently*) Oh yes.

ADE. And Gerald loves this countryside.

LOUIS. Helen is keen to have a change of air.

ADE. In that case, let's leave. It will be the first proof of my friendship for Helen. Because I do want us to be friends, Helen. (*to Louis*) Yes, we can have our revenge on you and Gerald. We'll have our own garret, Helen, just the two of us.

GERALD. (*to Louis*) Don't you tremble at the thought?

ADE. Then tremble! Helen, see you in the garret. Gerald, you come and help me pack our bags. (*As she leaves, she pulls Gerald out with her and sings.*)

> A drake spread out its wings one day,
> Quack, quack, quackety quack.
> Said he to his faithful duck, "I say,
> Quack, quack, quackety quack,
> When do you think we'll come to the end
> Of all our anguish and tears, my friend?"

LOUIS. They're so . . . what's the word . . . unpredictable.

HELEN. Yes.

LOUIS. Do you really believe her story? That she was just looking for a reason to come back to Gerald all that time she was with Achilles? And couldn't find any?

174

HELEN. Gerald believes it. That's all that matters.

LOUIS. Isn't it more important that she tell him the truth?

HELEN. You don't know how to pack a suitcase. Give me your ties.

LOUIS. Helen, I want to ask you something. It's quite trivial, really. (*pause*) Were you very fond of your parakeets?

HELEN. Yes, I was.

LOUIS. When he told you they were dead . . .

HELEN. If I'd had to choose between you and my parakeets, I'd still have chosen you. That's what you want to know, isn't it?

LOUIS. But you're rather upset about them, aren't you?

HELEN. Yes and no.

LOUIS. Have you often thought about them since we've been here?

HELEN. At their feeding time, I'd think about them sometimes.

LOUIS. Why didn't you tell me?

HELEN. They were very pretty. They knew me so well. Now, they are dead like so many other things I've known. Don't put your shoes on top of your shirts.

LOUIS. They're clean, and the shirts are filthy.

HELEN. I can't stand people saying they're right when they're wrong.

LOUIS. Come and kiss me.

(*Gerald enters and sees them in embrace.*)

GERALD. Everybody's happy, at last. Ade's wonderful. She thinks of everything. She even remembered about giving the laundry to the chambermaid.

HELEN. I'd forgotten about that. Better see her right away.

LOUIS. It doesn't matter if it's not ready. The hotel will send it on to us.

GERALD. What a rush! Anyone would think we were running away.

LOUIS. (*angrily*) Running away? What's there to run away from except your incessant bellyaching of the last few days?

GERALD. Let's not exaggerate. I was a little nervous, that's all. Helen, you are finally going to know me as I really am. I feel so on top of the world that if it rained, I'd still see the sun.

LOUIS. At this rate, we'll still be packing our bags tomorrow morning.

175

ADE. (*entering*) Hurry up, Gerald. You finish packing your own suitcases.

GERALD. You see, she agrees with you.

ADE. It's all too painful. Putting your things in the cases just as you did that day you were preparing to come here all by yourself. I keep seeing you there, cases open, looking around for me. How could you pack them? How could you leave without me?

GERALD. Louis, what do you bet tomorrow she'll be furious with me for leaving without her?

ADE. I can't help my simple nature. Come on, darling. (*sings*)

> Your turtledove has flown away
> Far, far away from you.
> But faithful she will ever stay
> And keep her promise true.

(*They exit.*)

LOUIS. Gerald is a complete fool.

HELEN. Why?

LOUIS. All this emotional outpouring for a lunatic wife who deceives him and returns like some innocent virgin.

HELEN. How do you know she deceived him?

LOUIS. You believe Ade?

HELEN. To tell you the truth, it's a matter of complete indifference to me. I'm more interested in my dead parakeets than in Ade's virtue.

LOUIS. I'm thinking about Gerald.

HELEN. That's why I say the main thing is that Gerald believe Ade's story.

LOUIS. Yes, but happiness based on a lie . . .

HELEN. Is there anything else you want to ask me, Louis?

LOUIS. Yes. That trip to Copenhagen, did you go there alone?

HELEN. No.

LOUIS. Who with?

HELEN. A man.

LOUIS. Was he your lover?

HELEN. Yes.

LOUIS. Was it like our trip to Pyla?

HELEN. I was hoping you wouldn't say that.

LOUIS. Do I know this man?

HELEN. No.

LOUIS. Do you still see him?

HELEN. No.

LOUIS. Were you still seeing him when I first met you?

HELEN. No. We never saw each other again after Copenhagen.

LOUIS. Why not?

HELEN. In the first place, because he lived there.

LOUIS. A Dane?

HELEN. Yes. Why not?

LOUIS. You wrote to him, then?

HELEN. No. I haven't given him a thought for months, and I don't know what's become of him.

LOUIS. Why did you never mention him before?

HELEN. Because when I'm alone or with you, I have no desire to remember him.

LOUIS. Well! That's all. I don't think I'll pack the bottle of polish.

HELEN. Just leave it.

LOUIS. It's half empty and might run out into the case — which wouldn't help things.

HELEN. Is that all you had to ask me?

LOUIS. Yes.

HELEN. Quite sure?

LOUIS. Quite sure, that is . . . apart from one or two little observations.

HELEN. Such as?

LOUIS. You know I don't have anything against mothers-in-law or cuckolds, and we rarely spoke about your husband.

HELEN. Yes.

LOUIS. But on the few occasions you did mention him, I imagined some sweet old man, a sort of dismal father who bored you to tears. But I was surprised. Your husband's a fine person, very distinguished, and far from being a doddering imbecile. He could be loved by any normal woman . . .

177

HELEN. He has talent and charm, I admit. But if the normal woman loves another man, how can she still love her husband?

LOUIS. What about the time you went to Copenhagen?

HELEN. Maybe I wasn't a normal woman, then.

LOUIS. And our first night together?

HELEN. The night after his father died?

LOUIS. Yes. When you stayed in Paris with me on the pretext of having a dress fitting or some such thing. I don't remember.

HELEN. Do you remember who's idea it was?

LOUIS. Mine. I think it was mine.

HELEN. You insisted we spend the whole night together to feel me sleeping beside you and watch me waking up.

LOUIS. Did you spend a whole night with that fellow in Copenhagen, too?

HELEN. Have you many more questions?

LOUIS. Not many, no.

HELEN. Let's get them over with.

LOUIS. What else did you expect? I didn't understand how things were, that night. My masculine selfishness was excusable.

HELEN. But you don't excuse me?

LOUIS. Of course, I excuse you.

HELEN. What else have you to ask me?

LOUIS. Is it true you were very affectionate towards your husband when you came back from Pyla?

HELEN. I've always felt a great affection for him.

LOUIS. What about me? Weren't you in love with me, then?

HELEN. What about you? Did you love me? Did you try to keep me when we came home? No, you dropped me at my husband's door, said, "See you tomorrow, darling," and off you went in your car.

LOUIS. So you're the kind of woman who can go away with a man you don't love!

HELEN. I'll go on with this strange interrogation — but on one condition — that you try to understand me. Yes, I loved you.

LOUIS. Like someone just passing through? Like the fellow in Copenhagen?

178

HELEN. Ask me your remaining questions and let's have an end of this.

LOUIS. Why did you tell me your husband was just a friend?

HELEN. If you'd had a little more courage, you'd have avoided that question.

LOUIS. You told me once you lived barricaded in your room.

HELEN. At the time, it was true.

LOUIS. And at other times?

HELEN. Louis, are we adding up a balance sheet or packing our bags? Mine are all ready.

LOUIS. Look at me, Helen . . .

HELEN. I am looking at you, Louis. I haven't taken my eyes off you all morning.

LOUIS. What is the matter with you?

HELEN. With me?

(*Enter Ade.*)

ADE. Finished.

LOUIS. (*shouting*) Finished? What's finished?

ADE. Our cases! I'm starving. Gerald's been telling me about a wonderful little restaurant near here, famous for its lemon-flavored teal. He's taking us all there for dinner.

GERALD. (*entering*) Why are you always running away from me? (*awkward pause*) Let's not search for hidden meanings in everything or life will become unbearable. No hidden meanings, even if the words seem to be making fun of us. I was saying, since you came back, you are always going off somewhere. And I need you so much now.

ADE. And I need you.

GERALD. Well then, come and help me.

ADE. I'm coming. (*Gerald exits.*) I'm so happy. I adore Gerald. He suffered so terribly when I was away.

LOUIS. What about the other poor devil? Aren't you itching to see him in agony now you've deserted him?

ADE. What poor devil? Achilles? He's a child. Too naive to know how to love. Besides, he never talked about it. Try to under-

179

stand, Louis. An elopement only lasts one night. After that, it's just another humdrum life starting all over again.

LOUIS. So now you admit you ran away with him.

ADE. Of course. I told you as much. We even traveled around together.

LOUIS. What if he'd killed Gerald, this morning?

ADE. Killed Gerald?

LOUIS. With your revolver.

ADE. (*laughing*) My revolver? Oh, how funny! You thought it was loaded? I'm not that crazy. It was empty.

LOUIS. Just like your heart.

ADE. What do you mean?

HELEN. Don't upset yourself, Louis. It's a good story.

LOUIS. I need her to love Gerald. I don't want to believe his happiness or misery depends on a liar.

ADE. Liar? Me? Well, there's nothing like being frank!

LOUIS. Didn't you lie? Either to Gerald or Achilles?

ADE. Never.

LOUIS. Didn't you tell me Achilles was your lover?

ADE. How could I say such a stupid thing, today of all days?

LOUIS. Not today but the day you left.

ADE. Stop being difficult, Louis. My poor Helen, you are in love with such a complicated man. Certainly I'm a changeable person like many other women. I change direction from one hour to the next, just like a bird, but I don't lie.

LOUIS. Don't talk to me about birds . . .

HELEN. Calm yourself, Louis.

ADE. Don't apologize for him. I love his violence because I love life. I love life so much I could live three lives, no four, five lives at the same time just like you when you had both your husband and Louis. But alas, I live quite simply, always treading a straight line. Of course, I sometimes change from one line to another and sometimes the lines come together. When that happens, I waver just for a moment, then I recover again.

LOUIS. What about the other people? Do they recover?

180

ADE. What others call my lies are my truths of the previous day or of my other existences. Do you understand?

LOUIS. No I don't. I only have one existence. Your system of separate compartments is too easy.

ADE. But when you tell a woman you love her, don't you ever remember saying it to other women? Is that not lying? Oh, you men! I am sure Helen wouldn't agree with you.

HELEN. When will we stop judging each other?

LOUIS. Were you Achilles' mistress? Yes or no?

ADE. (*indignant*) Me, Gerald's wife? Certainly not! (*Gerald enters.*) Darling! Stop Louis saying all these horrid things to me!

GERALD. What things?

HELEN. Louis is anxious to leave. Our bags are all packed. (*The telephone rings.*)

ADE. Telephone!

LOUIS. If this is another of your little tricks . . .

GERALD. (*to Louis, having taken the receiver*) It's for you, old boy. (*into receiver*) Who's speaking? It's personal. (*to Louis*) You want to take it? (*to Helen*) It's a man's voice.

ADE. That's no comfort. It's not women she's afraid of, is it Helen?

LOUIS. (*into receiver*) I understand perfectly. So urgent? Well . . . wait a minute. (*to the others*) Would you mind going into your room with Helen?

ADE. Of course not.

GERALD. Will you be long?

LOUIS. Ten minutes. (*into receiver*) Come up by the terrace. I'll meet you there. All right. (*hangs up*)

ADE. Are you coming, then, Helen?

HELEN. (*to Louis*) Promise me it isn't him coming back again.

LOUIS. Who?

HELEN. My husband.

LOUIS. No.

HELEN. He'll think up anything to separate us. You don't know him. Beneath the debonair exterior, he's a terrible man. He knows exactly what he wants. He knows how to worry you and still has a big hold over me.

181

LOUIS. A hold over you?

HELEN. Of course. He feels I'm still attached to him.

LOUIS. Attached? What do you mean?

HELEN. Oh! Don't misunderstand me. I'm going to stay.

LOUIS. It's not him anyway. And I've heard nothing about him except what you've just told me.

HELEN. I love you, Louis. I love you.

LOUIS. Trying to convince yourself?

HELEN. (*to Louis*) Tell me who it is.

LOUIS. Later.

ADE. (*to Helen*) He'll tell you later. Come on. Gerald. (*They exit.*)

LOUIS. (*shuts the door, goes onto the terrace, calls*) In here. Yes, that's right. Come in.

(*Enter Achilles.*)

ACHILLES. Thank you.

LOUIS. What do you want?

ACHILLES. Ade is here, with her husband, isn't she?

LOUIS. Yes.

ACHILLES. Do you know what she intends to do?

LOUIS. I don't see why I should tell you. This morning, I saw you with a gun in your hand.

ACHILLES. But I know you very well. Ade's been telling me all about you for four months now. You'd be surprised at what I know. Oh, insignificant things; for example, you don't like green ties.

LOUIS. For four months, you say?

ACHILLES. Yes, ever since I became Ade's lover.

LOUIS. You are Ade's lover?

ACHILLES. Didn't Ade tell you the day we ran off together so you could explain why she was leaving?

LOUIS. You sounded so desperate on the phone, I'm sure you aren't here to tell me I hate green ties and that you've been making love to my friend's wife for the past four months.

ACHILLES. After my visit this morning, I met Ade downstairs, and she asked me to wait for her at our hotel. But when I arrived there, the doorman told me she had left instructions for her bags to be brought here. I don't understand.

LOUIS. Why come to me for an explanation?

ACHILLES. I called her just now. She had a man answer the phone, her husband perhaps. I forgot to mention, her cases were all packed because we were leaving for Corsica this evening. I assume she doesn't intend going now. But why?

LOUIS. I've been living in a madhouse for the last little while. They talk of love, happiness, sorrow, all in the same breath. Are you a liar, too?

ACHILLES. I don't believe so.

LOUIS. Yet you deceived my friend; you lied like the rest of them.

ACHILLES. But I didn't know him.

LOUIS. You were party to a lie.

ACHILLES. What lie?

LOUIS. You heard a woman saying, "I love you" while she was repeating the same words to someone else.

ACHILLES. Who?

LOUIS. Her husband, of course.

ACHILLES. She didn't love him. Ade kept telling me all the time . . .

LOUIS. Naturally.

ACHILLES. What do you mean, "naturally"?

LOUIS. Ade swore she didn't love her husband, only you.

ACHILLES. She adored me. She took all sorts of risks for me. You know your garret . . .

LOUIS. First my green ties, now the garret. You know about that too?

ACHILLES. Yes, she took me there.

LOUIS. After we left Paris, I suppose?

ACHILLES. No. Before that. The day we went away, in fact, about six in the evening. She didn't know how to tell her husband she was leaving him and tried her hardest to be caught with me there. Would you like me to describe the garret?

LOUIS. No. I believe you.

ACHILLES. There is such a thing as truth, you see. Tell me, did she come home out of duty?

183

LOUIS. (*avoiding the question*) This is a hotel.

ACHILLES. I wanted to avoid saying "to the arms of her husband."

LOUIS. I don't think it was out of duty.

ACHILLES. When we got back from the casino, last night, Ade was never more tender, more loving. She loved the fragrance of the cool night air, the white clouds. She wouldn't sleep. She kept telling me I was the only man she had ever loved, but that she also wanted her husband's forgiveness so that nothing would mar her happiness.

LOUIS. So you came to ask for Gerald's forgiveness . . .

ACHILLES. . . . so that she could leave with me for our holiday, forgiven and without regrets.

LOUIS. The bitch.

ACHILLES. What?

LOUIS. They are all the same.

ACHILLES. What do you mean, "all"?

LOUIS. They are all mad, my poor friend, and Ade no more than the rest. She insisted you were merely a traveling companion.

ACHILLES. And her husband believed it?

LOUIS. Of course! When a man is alone with a woman and he's decided to believe everything she says, the idea she might be lying never enters his head.

ACHILLES. But why would she lie to me?

LOUIS. You are only a tool in her little game. We think we're their lovers, but we are only their accomplices.

ACHILLES. Ade was sincere. She gave me too many proofs of her love.

LOUIS. The damned liars! They are always sincere. That's why they can lie so well. My poor fellow, Ade is no different from the rest of them. She has always spoken the truth to everyone in succession while lying to everyone at the same time.

ACHILLES. But I saw her every day.

LOUIS. So did I.

ACHILLES. I telephoned her every morning.

LOUIS. Me, too.

184

ACHILLES. And if one day passed without her seeing me, she was completely miserable.

LOUIS. Same here. Really miserable.

ACHILLES. She even left her husband for me.

LOUIS. Same here.

ACHILLES. What do you mean, "same here"?

LOUIS. And she swore she no longer loved him.

ACHILLES. Yes.

LOUIS. They were just friends.

ACHILLES. Yes, just friends!

LOUIS. Same here. And when they tell us such things, they really believe them. They have no memory, no shame. For them it is true.

ACHILLES. You're not just saying this to protect your friend, are you? To keep me away from Ade?

LOUIS. (*angrily*) She's been telling him she adores him all morning. Doesn't that turn your stomach?

ACHILLES. Yes.

LOUIS. These women are not worth suffering for. But we have to pay for our stupidity. Would you care for some whisky?

ACHILLES. No thanks.

LOUIS. Don't you like it?

ACHILLES. Oh, yes.

LOUIS. You're not thirsty?

ACHILLES. I don't know. Though I admit this is a perfect time for a few whiskies, the mess we're in.

LOUIS. That's putting it mildly.

ACHILLES. And soon, it'll be worse. Give her back the revolver, will you. (*hands it over*)

LOUIS. There must surely be better things to do than waste our time with lunatic women. Life is short enough as it is.

ACHILLES. The tragedy, in fact, is that life is so short yet lasts so long.

LOUIS. (*banging his fists*) What fools we are! Women may have their charm but to entrust our happiness to them is utter madness.

185

ACHILLES. Yes. I hope for your sake you haven't lied.

LOUIS. What do you mean?

ACHILLES. These cases here . . .

LOUIS. They're ours. We were planning to leave together this evening, all four of us.

ACHILLES. Why the past tense?

LOUIS. Very well, we are leaving, definitely. And she certainly intends going with Gerald. Ade packed his bags herself!

ACHILLES. After packing mine?

LOUIS. That's right.

ACHILLES. Thanks for telling me.

LOUIS. Do you want me to give her any message?

ACHILLES. No. What's the point. I'll do it myself.

LOUIS. You must find this whole business rather painful.

ACHILLES. I'm humiliated. Oh, not in the way you think. I'm ashamed of myself. And what hurts me most is that her husband doesn't know she loved me; that she can tell him she never loved me. If only he could read her letters . . .

LOUIS. You're just saying anything that comes into your head as anyone would in your position. We suffer so we try to rationalize.

ACHILLES. Perhaps you're right. I'm in a daze. I just want to sleep.

LOUIS. Go and sleep, then. You'll feel a new man when you wake up.

ACHILLES. I should like to have lived with a woman like Ade, like the Ade I used to know.

LOUIS. You still want me to give her back the revolver?

ACHILLES. Why?

LOUIS. She said it was empty. (*looks*) She was right. I love symbolism. May I keep it?

ACHILLES. Please do. It's funny, I'm so nauseated, I don't feel grieved anymore. (*exits*)

LOUIS. Poor Achilles. Women! They're all the same. And to make matters worse, we're just as bad as they are. (*opens the door*) Helen. No. I'd like to see Helen alone. No. No trouble. Everything's perfect. (*Helen enters.*) Just like a shooting gallery where

186

the dummies are all in perfect position to be struck down one after another.

HELEN. You lied to me, of course.

LOUIS. Dear God, that's really funny.

HELEN. Was my husband here?

LOUIS. No. But he couldn't have been more interesting. Achilles just left. He really was Ade's lover.

HELEN. Did you doubt it?

LOUIS. I lacked experience, but I'm learning. It's a useless experience though, because once you've been through it, you don't want it anymore. What's the name of that dance where the women change partners when the music stops?

HELEN. Louis, let's go away from here and be on our own, just you and me.

LOUIS. In the village where I was born, a daughter of one of the farmers used to give herself to all the farmhands at harvesttime just for the pleasure of it. They used to call her "Summer Delight." Well, I wanted no part in such a fleeting love.

HELEN. You still love me, Louis?

LOUIS. How threatened people like you must feel when your love affairs break down and others see you as I do.

HELEN. Louis, when I was a young girl, I was as pure as you could want me. And if I'd met you when I was eighteen, I'd have given myself to you for the rest of my life. Oh, if only our life could begin now. (*pause*) For now, you can be sure I love you with all my heart and you alone.

LOUIS. Wonderful! Like a ship going down in a storm, and the captain saying, "Don't worry, men. We're still on the bridge."

ADE. (*entering*) Everything's ready. We are leaving for Paris after dinner. It's wonderful traveling at night, snuggled against the man you love, leaning back, looking at the sky and the stars.

GERALD. (*who has entered*) You know, since she came back, she's been living in a poet's dreamworld.

(*There is a gun shot.*)

LOUIS. A shot?

GERALD. Sounded like it. (*exits*)

ADE. How romantic men are. The porter drops a bag in the hall and they immediately think it's some crooked businessman saying goodbye to his associates.

(*Gerald comes back.*)

GERALD. Louis, here a minute.

HELEN. What is it?

GERALD. Nothing.

ADE. What did I tell you? He hasn't knocked over our trunks, I hope?

GERALD. Louis, quickly. (*to Ade and Helen*) You stay here. (*They exit.*)

ADE. I love Gerald when he's like this, so serious and tragic. He used to read his newspaper before, or tell me about Louis. That's why I nearly did something foolish.

HELEN. Nearly?

ADE. I risked losing a man who adores me. Helen, you dress delightfully. Did you buy your dress here?

HELEN. No. In Paris.

ADE. When you were with your husband? Did he like it?

HELEN. What are you driving at?

ADE. Your casino friend also dresses delightfully. Forgive me, I always say what I think.

HELEN. Your thoughts change so quickly. You don't have a very good memory, do you?

ADE. Neither do you, I hope. Because with your husband and Louis and a good memory, how could you manage not to think about one in front of the other?

HELEN. If Louis sees me as I see you, I can understand. Oh, God. I understand.

ADE. Understand what? (*Gerald and Louis re-enter.*) Where did you go?

GERALD. Come with me, Ade. Louis must speak to Helen alone.

ADE. Darling. (*to Helen and Louis*) See you soon. (*Ade and Gerald exit.*)

LOUIS. That young fellow just shot himself.

HELEN. Achilles?

LOUIS. In the hall, outside Ade's door. Just like that.

HELEN. Is he wounded? Or . . .

LOUIS. Yes. It's not very funny any more. Everything's becoming horrible.

HELEN. Then Gerald knows all about Achilles?

LOUIS. The poor kid. There was a note in his hand. A last will and testament. It said: "I really loved you." Nothing more. So I showed it to Gerald. He can go on believing quite happily in Ade's fantastic fairy tales.

HELEN. You see, there still are some true feelings left.

LOUIS. Which truth do you mean? There are so many varieties.

HELEN. Don't let Achilles or Jules destroy our happiness.

LOUIS. I'm responsible for what happened to Achilles. He thought I was speaking to him but I was only speaking to myself. He listened to me talking to myself. He pulled the trigger for me.

HELEN. Louis!

LOUIS. I've seen you lie too much.

HELEN. I lied for you.

LOUIS. No. You lied for both of us. Now I know how you give yourself to a passerby since I was one myself. It's our own actions which make me sick. I'm sick with myself.

HELEN. Louis, this is terrible. It's not fair.

LOUIS. I'll never forget what your husband said: "Some gigolo or other by the name of Louis Deshayes."

HELEN. You are too cruel, too vain, too selfish. You are so jealous and cowardly and frightened and full of anger . . .

LOUIS. And disgust.

HELEN. Oh! Goodbye.

(*She leaves by the terrace. Gerald enters by another door.*)

GERALD. I said nothing to Ade. What with her excessive temperament, I'll tell her later. Ask Helen not to mention it either.

LOUIS. Helen has gone.

GERALD. Where to?

LOUIS. Back to her husband, I imagine.

GERALD. What?

LOUIS. We're finished.

GERALD. Just like that? For nothing? So suddenly? (*Louis shakes his head.*) Come on, old boy, I'm with you. When I was miserable, you did everything to help me. Now it's my turn.

LOUIS. No. It's all over. I'll write to you.

GERALD. Where are you going?

LOUIS. I've no idea.

GERALD. (*calling*) Ade! Ade!

LOUIS. Our happiness sickened you. Yours is pitiful to me. So goodbye. I'm going into the desert to wait for the next generation. (*exits*)

GERALD. Louis!

ADE. (*entering*) What is it?

GERALD. Helen's left Louis.

ADE. Oh!

GERALD. She's gone back to her husband.

ADE. Oh! She's out of her mind.

GERALD. So Donaldo wasn't deceived after all. Their great love . . . was just a big joke.

ADE. A big joke? How sad.

CURTAIN

190

Marguerite

(LA MARGUERITE)

A PLAY IN ONE ACT BY
ARMAND SALACROU

ENGLISH VERSION BY NORMAN STOKLE

Characters in Order of Their Appearance

MARGUERITE, Paul's widow, 23 years old
DOCTOR, the family physician, 30 years old
OLD MAN, Paul's father, blind patriarch
VISITOR, a tramp, about 30 years old

The living room of a comfortably-off peasant family. On the walls are pictures of sea scenes. The furnishings include models of boats. To the right, a door leads out to the garden. At the back, another door leads to the rest of the house. It is evening. Soon, it will become dark outside. Marguerite, a young woman, is busy laying out a gentleman's black suit. The door at the back opens and a young doctor enters carrying his bag. He has just finished his consultation.

MARGUERITE. (*loudly so as to be heard by the sick old man at the end of the hall*) Well, doctor?

DOCTOR. (*in typical medical fashion*) Oh, he's coming along. (*closes the door*)

MARGUERITE. (*softly*) How is he?

DOCTOR. Blood pressure's still high. There's no change. He could continue like this for months or have another seizure and die within the hour.

MARGUERITE. (*wearily*) He's so worked up. He keeps calling for Paul. Paul, Paul, all the time. He knows Paul is dead, but he still waits for him to return. I feel completely exhausted tonight.

DOCTOR. I'll have to look after you next! (*pause*) What are you doing?

MARGUERITE. (*straightening out the black suit*) He made me clean Paul's black suit and lay it out for him.

DOCTOR. Oh, why?

MARGUERITE. He wants it to be all ready.

DOCTOR. Whatever for?

MARGUERITE. For Paul to wear. (*exasperated*) He thought his son would be coming home today. He has the strange idea that Paul will return exactly one hour before his last attack to help him die. So he wants Paul to wear this at the funeral. He told me to get it ready. He fingered it, smelt it . . .

DOCTOR. (*after a pause*) It's too early yet to begin the new series of injections.

MARGUERITE. Nothing settles him!

DOCTOR. My poor darling. I'll come back and see you after dinner.

MARGUERITE. I'll be waiting for you. But come in very quietly. He can hear a pin drop. You know how he gets up for the slightest little thing.

DOCTOR. I've forbidden him to get up.

MARGUERITE. He does exactly as he pleases. He's capable of anything.

DOCTOR. (*taking her in his arms*) You love me?

MARGUERITE. Oh! I don't know what I'd do without you. These last six months, I've been almost happy, thanks to you.

DOCTOR. Almost?

MARGUERITE. He's found out about us. How, I don't know.

DOCTOR. He knows we're in love?

MARGUERITE. Not exactly, but he suspects it.

DOCTOR. I'll be back straight after dinner.

MARGUERITE. All right, darling. Where are you going now?

DOCTOR. To Mrs. Pellerin's. Her boy has whooping cough.

MARGUERITE. Is there much of it going around?

DOCTOR. No.

MARGUERITE. Sssh! I can hear him walking about. Better go quickly.

DOCTOR. He's insane to get out of bed.

MARGUERITE. You know what he's like.

DOCTOR. Do what you can.

MARGUERITE. All right. Quickly.

DOCTOR. Till tonight, my darling.

MARGUERITE. Yes. Tonight.

194

(*As the Doctor leaves, a tall old man, in his dressing gown, comes in through the other door. It is not obvious that he is blind.*)

OLD MAN. That you, Paul?

MARGUERITE. Why are you up again?

OLD MAN. I heard voices. Who was here?

MARGUERITE. The doctor's just left.

OLD MAN. He hung about long enough down here, didn't he?

MARGUERITE. He was writing out a new prescription for you.

OLD MAN. Liar! You're Paul's wife, Marguerite, and don't you forget it. Paul's wife.

MARGUERITE. The doctor says you're not well enough to get up like this whenever you feel like it.

OLD MAN. That horse doctor's a fool . . . and a few other things besides.

MARGUERITE. Would you like a little meat soup?

OLD MAN. No.

MARGUERITE. Can I get you anything?

OLD MAN. You think you can ease your conscience with a bowl of soup? You're better at making soup than being a faithful wife, I'll say that. But I'm tired of your soup.

MARGUERITE. The doctor says your blood pressure is much too high for you to . . .

OLD MAN. Blood pressure! Blood pressure! Baloney! Just because I can't read your thermometers you're all for having that doctor in every five minutes. Here, in Paul's house. Have you no shame?

MARGUERITE. If you won't go back to bed, at least sit down.

OLD MAN. Keep your hands off me! I've mistrusted women all through this bitch of a life. I had my fill of them before, I can tell you, when I still had my eyes. All kinds of them! Just like dogs, they were, all different breeds: small ones, fat matrons with flabby breasts down to their ankles, and one, I remember, with a face like a greyhound — just like a dog, she was. Right from when I was young, they'd come sniffing around me, same as you and your doctor. So I had one, then another, here, there, and everywhere, just by putting out my hand . . . and now

195

that my life is over, when I think of all them hags stinking out the cemetery, I feel like spitting, like tearing out my mouth in disgust.

MARGUERITE. There's no sense in working yourself up like this. Why don't you try and sleep?

OLD MAN. As for you, when Paul was here and I still had my eyes, I thought you were all right. Even when the young idiot was away, you seemed decent and honest. Yes, but you covered things up better than I could keep my eyes on you. That's right, isn't it?

MARGUERITE. No, father.

OLD MAN. Father! I'm Paul's father, not yours. And just because those lying bastards say he's dead . . .

MARGUERITE. Quiet now.

OLD MAN. Quiet yourself. How could he be dead? Him? He took a few risks with his life, maybe. All right. Maybe he did. 'Cos I don't know much about life at sea. But he's not dead. And you, you're just like all the rest of them. Women! Silly bitches. That's what you are, the lot of you. Paul is coming back, I tell you. Because I know he is. Drowned! My son drowned! Ha!

MARGUERITE. Don't start again, for pity's sake.

OLD MAN. I'll have pity when he comes home. I didn't want Paul to be a sailor. You know that. But he wanted to go. And as he's more pigheaded than me, he had his way. But he's not drowned, I tell you. He'll be back. Sons have no right to die before their fathers. Me, I'm pigheaded too. I won't die before he gets here. I'll wait for him.

MARGUERITE. Don't tire yourself so. Try to keep calm.

OLD MAN. I am calm. Very calm. I'm waiting for my son to bring some order into this house. When he gets home, I'll be off. That'll suit me fine, because don't think I enjoy being here. I've had enough of your tantrums. (*pause*) You ought to be ashamed of yourself, making up to that little crab of a doctor. (*Marguerite tries to interrupt.*) I've never seen him with my eyes, but he talks like a crab, I tell you, like a crab walking on the bottom of the sea. (*imitates walk with his hands*) That's how he talks!

196

MARGUERITE. You're perspiring.

OLD MAN. Three years! Couldn't you wait three years?

MARGUERITE. For what?

OLD MAN. (*triumphantly*) Him. And you were such a decent sort of a girl before. You loved your husband. Couldn't you wait for him? But you didn't really love Paul.

MARGUERITE. (*violently*) Then who else? Who else?

OLD MAN. No. You loved a man, that's all. Any man. You've always got to have a man in your bed, or out in the fields, or by the roadside. Miserable wretches, that's what you are.

MARGUERITE. (*indignant, but controlled*) You have no right to speak to me like this.

OLD MAN. (*letting himself go*) I had a woman in the mud one night. Yes, in the mud, in the pouring rain. Ha! You're a pretty sight with your legs kicking in the air, oh, a pretty sight, I can tell you. You made me laugh, the lot of you, with your legs up in the air.

MARGUERITE. (*who can stand no more*) Excuse me please. I have to leave you a moment. I'm worried about my son. He hardly ate a thing this evening. He seems a little feverish and I'm frightened in case he uncovers himself while he's asleep . . . especially with all this whooping cough about.

OLD MAN. I never asked you to stay with me. Go and leave me to die here. Besides, I won't die. I'm waiting for Paul. A fine lad, he was. Strong. Tough. He was strong, right enough, my Paul. I still had my eyes, last time he went away. Now, I'll never see him again, but I'll hear his voice. So Paul's ship went down. Fine, it's sunk; I'm the first to admit it. They say it went down very fast; quite possible. But just because you sleep with a horse doctor, that doesn't make Paul a fool. The sea . . . why it's not like the desert. You can live in the sea. There's fish, to start with. Maybe it looks like nothing, but it proves something to me. And there's roads on the sea, just like in the forests. Where one boat crosses, another boat can cross back again. And there's my Paul on the bridge. The boat is heading back to port where there's railways . . . Yes! Listen. (*A train whistle is heard in the distance.*) The fourteen minutes past eight. That's the train.

197

Who's to say Paul's not on it? He's getting off. That old fool Prevost collects his ticket, recognizes him. "Why it's Paul! Our own Paul! But hurry . . . run quickly . . . quickly." Listen. I thought I heard the garden gate.

MARGUERITE. Calm yourself, for both our sakes.

OLD MAN. (*opening door leading to the road and calling into the night*) Paul! Paul! That you? No. He won't be coming tonight.

MARGUERITE. Every hour of the day and night for three long years you've been trying to save Paul from shipwreck.

OLD MAN. And I'll bring him back wherever he is, North, South, East, or West. And one day, you'll see him too, standing right there in front of you. The young devil!

(*There is the sound of a clock striking.*)

MARGUERITE. You really ought to be in bed.

OLD MAN. No.

MARGUERITE. It's time for your medicine. And you must take it in bed.

OLD MAN. Not that I think you want to poison me!

MARGUERITE. Oh!

OLD MAN. (*softly*) Because you daren't. You haven't the courage, either of you. All you can do is hide in your room and draw the curtains to hide yourselves even from the light — you and your doctor!

MARGUERITE. Excuse me. I must go and see to my son.

OLD MAN. (*violently*) But you forget, my blind eyes can see in the dark. (*Marguerite has exited.*) Her son! Her son! How can the good Lord expect me to take a strange woman and a newborn child in place of my own boy? If Paul had been here, maybe I could have put up with the pair of them. A man needs a wife and kids. But that little brat can't even remember his father and looks like him less and less. And her, carrying on with that doctor. Doctor he calls himself! Huh! Sniffing away at my ailments! He thinks I'm dead already. But I'll show him. I'm not dying. All right, so Paul's ship went down, sank, I don't deny it. And very fast. Quite possible. Front went down, back came up. And the ship plunged into the sea like so; like a knife in the belly of an old woman. Yes, all right. Then what? Wouldn't Paul have thought about me? Would he have just let himself slip down with it, right to the bottom? Why that's ridiculous. Once in the water, he came back up to the surface where there was air to breathe. It was calm, they told me. He must have kept afloat on a piece of wood. Don't kid me everything goes to the bottom, even in the worst catastrophes. Then something came by and picked him up. God only knows where he went to! Where the rescue ship was going, I suppose. And, by Heaven, that was where the fun started. Paul, you young devil! What adventures you must have had! Some beauties, I bet! I can just see him tickling those Chinese girls. What a lad! Oh, but when he gets back, I'll tell him what's on my mind. He doesn't know about my eyes yet. But he knows I'm old. And I've had enough waiting around for him. I want to be off. I'm weary. From China, it shouldn't be all that difficult to get back here. How would he go? I don't know! But there must be some sort of a road, surely. Oh, I know. He must have got sick of the sea . . . so he heads for home, going from town to town and stopping off at all the pubs. And he feels a little wicked smiling at the barmaids when all the time his Marguerite is getting the treatment from her doctor friend. If only I knew where to write to him. He's a crafty one, he is. Having such a good time, he goes and hides himself. But Paul, what's keeping you, son? You know you have to come back here in the end. My young Paul, now you listen to me. Take the fourteen minutes past eight train. That old idiot Prevost'll take your ticket at the barrier and suddenly, he'll recognize you: "Why, it's the old man's boy, it's Paul . . . Hurry . . . better run, your father's waiting for you. Maybe he's going to die tonight . . . Hurry, your black suit is all ready. Run, Paul . . . Your old dad isn't feeling so good." And Paul runs without even stopping to take his bearings. There's the school and Father Garnier's rambling old house and the church whose bells will toll tomorrow for your old father. Hurry, Paul. I hear you running along the road. You're home. You push open the garden gate. (*noise of small bells on gate*) It rings. Just a few

199

steps more and you open the door. (*The door from the garden opens.*) Oh! And not before time. I couldn't have held out any longer.

(*A very shabbily dressed man, obviously tired and anxious, enters.*)

OLD MAN. Hurry, my boy, come in, come in.

VISITOR. (*disconcerted*) Good evening.

OLD MAN. (*furious*) "Good evening"! Is that all you can find to say?

VISITOR. (*bewildered*) Yes.

OLD MAN. Fantastic! Fantastic! You open the door, come in and say, "Good evening" as if you'd only been away five minutes.

VISITOR. I've traveled a long way.

OLD MAN. Oh! I should just think you have!

VISITOR. And I'm tired.

OLD MAN. You shouldn't have loafed about so much on the way. But if you're tired, I'll let you sit down.

VISITOR. Thank you.

OLD MAN. You don't sound very proud of yourself.

VISITOR. I have no cause to be!

OLD MAN. (*suddenly becoming aware of the Visitor's presence*) But it's really you! (*violently*) Tell me, is it you answering me?

VISITOR. (*taken aback*) All I said was, "I have no cause to be proud of myself."

OLD MAN. (*calling*) Marguerite! Marguerite! Paul's home! Paul's come back to us. He's here. Paul! Now I can die. (*He collapses. The Visitor supports him.*)

VISITOR. Careful now! Steady! Wait a minute. Poor old man.

(*Marguerite enters.*)

MARGUERITE. Lord save us. What has happened?

VISITOR. I don't know.

MARGUERITE. (*bringing a chair for the Old Man*) Give me a hand.

VISITOR. I came in here because I wanted food. This isn't my fault.

MARGUERITE. I heard him shouting, "Paul's home"!

VISITOR. That's right.

MARGUERITE. But you came by yourself, didn't you? Didn't you?

200

VISITOR. (*thinking himself under suspicion*) Don't worry. I'm alone, all right.

MARGUERITE. His heart's pounding like a hammer. He's having trouble with his breathing.

OLD MAN. (*coming to*) Marguerite, I dreamt that . . . (*He seizes the Visitor's hand.*) Ah! Paul . . . my son! My son! Get me something to drink, Marguerite. (*to the Visitor*) Where have you been so long, you young delinquent?

VISITOR. Where have I been?

OLD MAN. Yes.

VISITOR. Tramping the roads.

MARGUERITE. If you could see him, father . . .

OLD MAN. (*angrily*) Do you think I need to be reminded I can't see him? Don't you know my heart is heavy enough just hearing his voice and not being able to see him?

MARGUERITE. What I meant was . . .

OLD MAN. What?

MARGUERITE. He looks very tired.

OLD MAN. Don't tell me you came all the way back on foot?

VISITOR. Yes, I did.

OLD MAN. (*taken aback*) Oh! (*drinks*) You've had a hard time of it then, eh?

VISITOR. Yes.

OLD MAN. Why didn't you write?

(*The Visitor looks questioningly at Marguerite. She makes an evasive gesture.*)

VISITOR. I'll tell you about it later.

OLD MAN. Do you see much change in Marguerite?

(*Marguerite gestures.*)

VISITOR. No.

OLD MAN. What about me?

(*Marguerite gestures.*)

VISITOR. You haven't changed much.

OLD MAN. So you've had some hard times, then?

VISITOR. You can say that again.

OLD MAN. Tell me quickly. Was it in them seas around China where they picked you up?

(*Marguerite gestures.*)

VISITOR. China? That's a good one. (*laughs*) China?

OLD MAN. (*irritated*) Was it around China or wasn't it?

VISITOR. (*calming him*) Yes, China.

OLD MAN. A fine how-d'you-do, that is! I must say. Being a sailor so you could throw yourself to the fishes. But I'll tell you what I think of you later. Do you still hit the bottle as hard as ever?

(*There is an evasive gesture from Marguerite.*)

VISITOR. Yes.

OLD MAN. And were you stinking with liquor when your ship went down?

(*Marguerite does not reply to the Visitor's gesture.*)

VISITOR. No, I wasn't.

OLD MAN. Then why did you sink your ship? (*Marguerite and the Visitor exchange perplexed glances.*) Why did you sink your ship?

VISITOR. These things happen in the navy.

OLD MAN. Good job I'm not deaf in my ears. 'Cos when I told you that same thing before, you just laughed in my face.

VISITOR. (*amused*) I did? (*laughs slightly*)

OLD MAN. Damned idiot. Marguerite, give me some more water. I'm thirsty.

MARGUERITE. You mustn't drink too much . . .

OLD MAN. (*to Marguerite*) That's enough out of you! Do as I say. (*to Visitor*) You know something, Paul, I've worked pretty hard in my time. A lot more than you know about. But I never sweated so hard before just to keep hanging onto life until you came back. During the night, sometimes, to keep my spirits up a bit, I kept thinking you must be having one hell of a struggle yourself hanging onto your life in the middle of the ocean. (*Marguerite gives him a glass of water.*) Thanks, Marguerite.

MARGUERITE. (*to the Visitor, with great difficulty*) Paul . . . tell your father to go to bed.

VISITOR. (*uncomprehending*) What?

202

MARGUERITE. Tell your father to go to bed.

OLD MAN. No. I want Paul to give the orders here. But when I'm dead, not before.

VISITOR. (*to Old Man*) Sit down, you'll feel better.

OLD MAN. Is my blindness very noticeable?

(*Marguerite gestures.*)

VISITOR. No.

OLD MAN. Are my eyes the same?

VISITOR. Just the same.

OLD MAN. Imagine! I can't even see my eyes any more! Tomorrow, I'll be all dead, the whole lot, ears included. And that suits me fine. It's hard, not being master of your own body no matter what you do. Marguerite kept telling me my eyes were just the same . . . with the same color. So it's true after all. I can believe you, Paul. (*to Marguerite*) Has he changed much?

MARGUERITE. Yes.

OLD MAN. How is he?

MARGUERITE. Tomorrow . . .

OLD MAN. What do you mean! Tomorrow?

MARGUERITE. (*with effort*) He's clean-shaven now.

OLD MAN. Why did you cut off your beard?

VISITOR. (*after looking at Marguerite*) Because . . . one day . . . I had to.

OLD MAN. Did you have to go into hiding on your way home?

VISITOR. Something like that.

OLD MAN. Did you do something bad?

VISITOR. My life wasn't exactly easy.

OLD MAN. My poor boy! But you didn't do anything bad around here, did you. Not in the neighborhood, for Heaven's sake?

VISITOR. No, not around here. Further afield.

OLD MAN. Oh, in China, was it? Well . . . if you did it in China, I couldn't care less! Damn good thing, in fact, doing it in China! Ha! Ha! That's my boy! Oh, if you only knew how frustrating it is being respectable all your life. I wanted to let off steam plenty of times, I can tell you. Let my hair down in my own way. And I was afraid to, because of the neighbors — who are all dead now. But if I could have gone to China! Tell me about it. Come on, out with it. (*with joyful pride*) You young devil!

VISITOR. I didn't mean to be so stupid, but I sort of got mixed up in things. One thing led to another. You know how it is.

OLD MAN. Oh, you were never one for talking. Paul . . .

VISITOR. Yes.

OLD MAN. Let me touch your face with my hands.

VISITOR. No. I don't go for that.

OLD MAN. But since I can't see you any more . . .

VISITOR. Let another man put his hands on my face! Oh, no.

OLD MAN. Another man! I'm your father.

VISITOR. My father? What is all this? My father?

OLD MAN. Yes, your father!

VISITOR. (*deciding to go*) Oh! I've had enough.

OLD MAN. (*irritated*) What's this?

MARGUERITE. (*very gently*) Paul, Paul.

VISITOR. (*calming down*) Look, I'm hungry.

MARGUERITE. Yes, right away. I've some bread, some cold meat, and . . .

OLD MAN. No. Three whole years I've been waiting for him, day after day. Now I have to talk to him. He can eat when I've said my say. Leave us, Marguerite.

VISITOR. I can listen while I'm having a bite to eat.

OLD MAN. For the love of God! Just because I can't see, that doesn't mean I'm not still head of this house tonight. Tomorrow, I may be a stinking corpse, but tonight, I'm still the master around here. Leave us, Marguerite. (*Marguerite opens and closes the door but remains motionless inside the room and looks at the Visitor. She will indicate, through gestures, certain replies to him.*) Sit yourself down. (*Visitor sits.*) Are you sat down?

VISITOR. Yes.

(*Old Man goes to check with his hands.*)

OLD MAN. Good. Do you plan going away again?

(*Marguerite indicates "No."*)

VISITOR. No.

OLD MAN. Good. The farm's been looked after in the way you might expect it to be, by a sick old man and a weak slip of a girl. Now it's your job to look after things and be the master.

VISITOR. That would be just fine with me.

OLD MAN. Then I did well to wait for you. I can die more peacefully. Though Heaven knows why, because everything disgusts me. Maybe I'm just tired. After all, why should I worry my head about what's going to happen on the earth when I'll soon be six feet under it? Tell me that?

VISITOR. (*laughing*) Yes, it's sort of funny, isn't it.

OLD MAN. You've come back from the dead so you should be able to tell me.

VISITOR. We think we understand at the time. Then when it's all over, we don't know any more.

OLD MAN. But when you were struggling under the water, did you think you'd get out alive, or be stuck there for good?

VISITOR. When you are capsizing, you don't usually think about anything.

OLD MAN. How is that?

VISITOR. Words can't explain it.

OLD MAN. But did you want to be saved? Did you want to reach dry land or not?

VISITOR. (*chaffingly*) Well, by choice, myself, I prefer terra firma, because when everything starts giving way around you, you've still got your feet on the ground. That doesn't give way, at least.

OLD MAN. (*violently*) Serves you right! If I hadn't been waiting for you, I wouldn't have cared if you'd rotted away in the water. It wasn't easy waiting for you hour after hour. An hour's a long time, but it doesn't take up much room in a whole day, or a day in a month, or a month in a year, and all that waiting, hour after hour.

VISITOR. Yes. Hey look, I'm starving.

OLD MAN. You'll eat when I tell you. Now tell me about Marguerite.

VISITOR. What do you want me to say?

OLD MAN. You still love her?

VISITOR. (*looks at Marguerite*) She's a nice girl.

OLD MAN. What does that mean? What do you think love is?

VISITOR. She's even quite beautiful.

OLD MAN. Take care. Beauty is a trap, an obsession that distracts a man from his work.

VISITOR. Doing what?

OLD MAN. Are you still as bullheaded as ever? That's why you went to sea, remember! So as not to work on the farm.

VISITOR. I don't deny it. But she is beautiful.

OLD MAN. Beautiful! Beautiful! Sometimes that's the very thing that stops a man from being happy.

VISITOR. Oh, happiness! My mother used to say, "Happiness is not of this world."

OLD MAN. (*surprised*) Your mother said that? She never said it to me. (*gesture from Marguerite*) Poor woman! (*pause*) Happiness is not of this world? She told you that, eh? What had she to complain about? Did you ever hear me complaining? Never! Only, your gadding about all over the place for three years wasn't very bright. Everything needs building up again on the farm. You'll have to straighten things out. You didn't speak to me much about Marguerite in the old days. But I had my eyes. You loved her as a wife should be loved. There was no nonsense. What about now?

VISITOR. What about it?

OLD MAN. Are you jealous?

VISITOR. What of?

OLD MAN. What did you think about when you were struggling in the water?

VISITOR. In the water?

OLD MAN. Yes.

VISITOR. Well, what are you thinking about right now?

OLD MAN. What do you mean?

VISITOR. (*chaffingly*) Aren't you struggling in the water yourself?

OLD MAN. (*violently*) Don't mention water to me. It's terrified me for three years now. I won't be able to breathe when I'm under

206

the ground, and I don't gasp, thinking about it. But when I think of the ocean depths, I feel like choking because of you.

VISITOR. I've had enough. I don't like talking about death all the time.

OLD MAN. Why not?

VISITOR. It makes me want to . . .

OLD MAN. Want to what?

VISITOR. (*violently*) Want to do what they did — and say goodbye to it all. I was hungry when I came here and I am still. Well, maybe it sounds silly, but I feel like eating and dying at the same time.

OLD MAN. You want a good clip on the head? So you're hungry? All right. If I keep you waiting, I have my reasons. I'm still the boss around here. How can you talk of dying at your age?

VISITOR. Were you happy at my age?

OLD MAN. Happy? What does that mean?

VISITOR. Happy, like everyone else, like other people.

OLD MAN. You big donkey! You live your daytime, and your nighttime, then more daytime and more nighttime, and so it goes on till it's all over.

VISITOR. Maybe you're right. But I come here tonight, and you don't know a thing about me.

OLD MAN. Not any more, I don't. You've been away so long. And now, I can't even see you to guess the meaning of what you say.

VISITOR. (*disillusioned*) Oh, the things people say to each other!

OLD MAN. We never had much to say to each other, you and me. I didn't like that, and neither did you. Well now, I'm saying my last words. I remember the day you were born. Your mother was resting. Heaven knows she had cause to. "Happiness is not of this world," she said that, eh? I wouldn't have believed it. Not a day old, you were, and I carried you in my arms and showed you all around the farm; introduced you to the animals. Remember the old horse I had, called . . . er . . . what was his name? . . . Oh well, nobody will ever know what he was called now. You were no bigger than my fist. You didn't even laugh. You were never one for making a fuss, and I was proud of

207

you. "Look at our apple trees," I said, "look at the fine crop of oats, and the dogs, and the cats, and the fat sow grunting away." And I shouted, "Here's the young baby, here's my little boy." The sun was shining . . . and I can't remember any more. All my days have been long ones and my life has gone so quickly. But now, you are home again. I wanted to say a word about Marguerite . . . (*a silence*)

VISITOR. What about Marguerite?

OLD MAN. We had a quarrel one day about her, the only time you ever mentioned her to me. Remember?

VISITOR. What if I do?

OLD MAN. 'Course you remember. You had funny eyes that day. And you said, "Marguerite is the only thing in the world that matters to me." So I said, "Why don't you stay on at the farm now you're married?" "Because I know she can wait for me," you said. "But why do you want to leave her if you think so much about her?" I said. "Stay with the farm." "I need a change of air," you said, "and when I'm far away, I'm still close to her. She's always in my thoughts." Damn little fool! Then, what was it you said? "I'm only going away so I can think about her better. Then I'll come home and see her again and we'll love each other more than ever."

VISITOR. (*sadly*) I said that?

OLD MAN. Your very words. Then off you went to spend three years with those Chinese women, you damned fool. You thought better about her all right! (*Marguerite has heard all this. She cries. Then she opens and closes the door to signify her "entry."*) That you, Marguerite?

MARGUERITE. Yes, father.

OLD MAN. How's the boy?

MARGUERITE. Asleep.

OLD MAN. Well, don't you think you should wake him up . . . on the day his father returns from the bottom of the sea?

MARGUERITE. It might be wiser just . . .

OLD MAN. Here's me talking away about my own son all the time, and Paul couldn't care less about my son. It's his own son he's interested in.

VISITOR. You're right there.

OLD MAN. Go and have a look at him.

VISITOR. Me?

OLD MAN. Of course, you.

VISITOR. My son? It's not possible. I can't do it.

OLD MAN. Why not? He's in his room. The one you painted all in white, and you sang all the time doing it, remember, Marguerite? Go up and see him. I'll let you. I'll live till you come down again. Marguerite will stay with me. (*Marguerite and the Visitor exchange signs. The Visitor exits.*) Well, Marguerite, are you proud of yourself now Paul's home?

MARGUERITE. If only you'd stay quiet!

OLD MAN. I've said nothing to Paul. Not for your sake, but for his. There are times a man needs his wife. Not often, but sometimes. So, what about your doctor friend now, eh?

MARGUERITE. I beg you to be quiet.

OLD MAN. Begging me now, are you! Afraid in case I tell Paul everything! Or are you ashamed? Then it was true about you and your doctor? Tell me! I can hardly believe it now Paul is home again. But if I ever hear anything about you and that doctor, even if I'm dead and buried, I'll climb out of my grave and throttle you.

(*A silence. The Doctor enters quietly, sees the Old Man is up and decides to speak.*)

DOCTOR. You are not being fair to yourself.

OLD MAN. What's that?

MARGUERITE. It's the doctor.

DOCTOR. Out of bed again! A fine patient you are! What are you doing in here, eh?

OLD MAN. And yourself?

DOCTOR. Oh, I was just passing, and I saw the light on. And I've been a little worried about you. Give me your hand. (*feels the pulse*) Yes. Just as I thought.

OLD MAN. What is it?

209

DOCTOR. (*still trying to understand Marguerite's new attitude*) I've told you a hundred times, your blood pressure is extremely high. You've had two minor strokes already and I can't start you on your new series of injections yet. We have to wait awhile. The left arm is swelling, you know that. You must try and control your excitement. You are not being reasonable.

OLD MAN. Are you reasonable?

DOCTOR. (*shocked*) Me?

OLD MAN. Give me your pulse. (*feels for it*) Where do you press to hear the heartbeat?

DOCTOR. (*trying to laugh it off*) Do you want to take my temperature or check my arteries?

OLD MAN. Yes.

DOCTOR. Here it is. That's it.

OLD MAN. Don't feel a thing. But maybe I'll feel something now. Paul's come back.

DOCTOR. (*disbelievingly*) Paul's come back? What are you trying to tell me?

OLD MAN. (*triumphant*) Yes, my boy is home again.

DOCTOR. (*calming him*) He'll come home some day and you should look after yourself while you're waiting for him.

OLD MAN. Don't you think I've waited long enough!

DOCTOR. Keep hoping, but keep calm.

OLD MAN. "Keep hoping"! Ha! He's priceless, he is! Look, horse doctor, you didn't exactly bend over backwards to believe he was still alive, did you?

DOCTOR. (*astonished by Marguerite's attitude*) Tell me, Marguerite . . .

OLD MAN. Go on, tell him, Marguerite! I doubt if people on their deathbeds feel like praising their doctors very much, but you go one better than the rest. His patients aren't enough for him. He wants to bury the hale and hearty, as well.

DOCTOR. I insist you go and lie down.

OLD MAN. I'm through with your prescriptions. For Heaven's sake, he still doesn't believe me. Go on, tell him, Marguerite.

MARGUERITE. (*quietly*) It's true.

OLD MAN. He opened the door and came right in.

DOCTOR. Is this true, Marguerite?

OLD MAN. So, we have nothing to say to each other, you and me, and everything to learn. Don't think I had any confidence in your drugs. It was him I lived for.

DOCTOR. Listen to me.

OLD MAN. No. Doctors are like priests. You either believe them or you don't, but you still have to have them. Well, from now on, you're no use to me. It's the priest I need.

DOCTOR. How right you are! You are killing yourself.

OLD MAN. I have that right, now. Because Paul's home again with Marguerite. (*Marguerite has avoided looking at the Doctor throughout this scene. The Visitor enters.*) That you, Paul?

DOCTOR. (*flabbergasted*) Who is this, Marguerite?

OLD MAN. Who do you think it is! Paul, you've got your eyes. This is the doctor. He came to these parts after I took sick. He thought he was doing me some good. But now he'll have no more business coming here. I'm finished. I don't feel like lingering on any more and being a burden to you. Oh, I was forgetting, what do you think of your son? Here a minute. (*He touches the Visitor's face. The Visitor, deeply touched, lets him do so.*) You been crying?

VISITOR. Yes.

OLD MAN. And the boy. What did he say?

VISITOR. Nothing. He was asleep.

OLD MAN. You didn't wake him?

VISITOR. No. I watched him sleeping. He's as handsome as his mother.

OLD MAN. Doesn't he look like you?

VISITOR. Children always look like their mothers to begin with. I know how it is.

OLD MAN. Try and bring him up like I brought you up. Especially if he's as stubborn as you were. Well, doctor, what do you think of my Paul?

DOCTOR. (*not understanding the situation*) I advise you as a doctor, you'd be wise to go and rest.

211

OLD MAN. Soon, I'll have all the time in the world for rest — a long, long rest. Son, Marguerite has your black suit all ready. And while I think about it, you're not to get drunk at my funeral. I forbid it. Don't you get stoned, do you hear? And keep down the expenses with the priest. We didn't do all that well while you were gallivanting about in China. Spend less than when you were married, you young devil! Oh, doctor, if you had seen them married! You were lovely, Marguerite. I want to tell you that, to-night. I gave her my arm and I was proud. Proud! They were very much in love! Tell the doctor how much you loved her, Paul, so he knows, so he understands.

VISITOR. Understands what?

MARGUERITE. (*close to tears*) I was so happy, so happy.

OLD MAN. You know something, doctor, I wouldn't let them have a honeymoon. I didn't go for that. Why, I don't know. Then see-ing them kissing each other like that, my heart warmed and I told them right there in the middle of the wedding reception, I told them, "Take the horse and trap, my children, and come back in two weeks." Just like that. You remember, Marguerite?

MARGUERITE. Yes.

OLD MAN. "Two weeks," I said. I couldn't go back on my word. And off you went, straight away, without swallowing another bite, and you in your white dress! Paul, you never wanted to tell me where you both went.

MARGUERITE. To Combreville, a little village where I'd spent my holidays as a little girl.

OLD MAN. The whole two weeks?

MARGUERITE. Yes. The village was full of roses, and there were geraniums on our window ledge . . .

OLD MAN. Yes.

MARGUERITE. Every afternoon, we would walk in the forest.

OLD MAN. (*lewdly*) Aha! Well, well! I see! In the forest, eh? Paul, you young devil!

MARGUERITE. (*in tears*) Paul! Paul! Paul!

OLD MAN. Go on. Take her in your arms.

212

(*Between the two men who look at each other, Marguerite opens her arms and closes them around the empty air.*)

MARGUERITE. Paul!

OLD MAN. Well, my children, when I'm gone, I want you both to go back there for another two weeks. That's an order. Afterwards, you can come home and start work.

MARGUERITE. Yes, I'll go, I promise you.

OLD MAN. I was right, you see, to keep struggling on. Now, I can say my goodbyes and make a quick exit. Oh yes, they could all see you floating among the fishes and the seaweed, moving under the belly of floating islands, or lying there in the sand under the rocks like a drowned man. Oh! Oh! And you came back, as I said you would, striding across the land. (*He is seized by an attack.*)

DOCTOR. It was inevitable.

OLD MAN. It's nothing.

DOCTOR. I'm going to try . . .

OLD MAN. You'll try nothing. Just one thing I need. Give me your shoulder, my son, and let's go.

VISITOR. Where to?

OLD MAN. My room.

MARGUERITE. At the end of the hall.

DOCTOR. I must give you treatment. It's vital.

OLD MAN. No!

DOCTOR. You are in a critical condition. Very critical!

OLD MAN. Shut up! (*to Paul*) I'll be all right in bed. Sleeping near you.

MARGUERITE. I'll go first.

OLD MAN. You stay here. Paul knows the way.

VISITOR. Come on, then.

OLD MAN. Goodnight all, Goodbye, doctor. And don't forget, Marguerite, Paul's home now.

(*They exit, the Old Man supported by the Visitor.*)

DOCTOR. He's killing himself.

MARGUERITE. He gives the orders.

DOCTOR. (*after short pause*) Who is this man?

MARGUERITE. I don't know.

DOCTOR. Where does he come from?

MARGUERITE. I don't know.

DOCTOR. Did he know Paul?

MARGUERITE. I don't think so. No.

DOCTOR. Then what is all this hoax about?

MARGUERITE. What hoax?

DOCTOR. How could you allow a total stranger to take the place of your husband? Darling . . .

MARGUERITE. Don't touch me.

DOCTOR. Marguerite.

MARGUERITE. Don't you see? It could just as well have been Paul who opened that door tonight.

DOCTOR. For pity's sake! Don't tell me you are losing your senses too. Paul can't come back. You know that as well as I do.

MARGUERITE. But what I didn't know was that if he came back, I should throw myself into his arms and beg his forgiveness. That's what I didn't know — that I should rush into his arms. But would he still want to hold me? Would he want any part of me?

DOCTOR. What's the use of finding excuses for a man who can't come back?

MARGUERITE. I thought he was dead, but if he is alive, I can only love him. I'm so ashamed and sick at heart. How else can I feel?

DOCTOR. But he deserted you for months on end.

MARGUERITE. Now I know why.

DOCTOR. Why?

MARGUERITE. To think about me more clearly. About the woman he loved more than anything else in the world.

DOCTOR. You're dreaming! If he came through that door this minute, he'd be blind drunk, to start with. You said so yourself.

MARGUERITE. And me? What could I say to him?

DOCTOR. If he came back, he wouldn't be at all as you imagined him.

MARGUERITE. What do you know about it?

DOCTOR. This is ridiculous. You know very well he can't come back. He's dead.

MARGUERITE. If he is dead, then you can do nothing to hurt him. The living are the ones who change, who become evil, who grow old. But Paul will always be young and tender as he was the day he went away.

DOCTOR. You are talking nonsense.

MARGUERITE. No. Believe me, the living grow old and die, but the dead no longer grow old . . .

DOCTOR. (*ironically*) . . . and still live?

MARGUERITE. I'm sure all this must grieve you. But how could you hold me in your arms again, knowing that if Paul came back, I should break away from you and throw myself at his feet?

DOCTOR. Paul can't come back!

MARGUERITE. (*on her knees*) At his feet, like an unfaithful wife. Please forgive me, Paul, for being unfaithful; for deceiving you with this man I didn't love. It's you I love, you, my husband, and I beseech you to keep me close, if only to serve you.

(*The Visitor re-enters.*)

DOCTOR. Oh! So there you are.

(*Marguerite rises quickly.*)

VISITOR. (*brutally*) Give me something to drink.

DOCTOR. A fine mess you've made!

VISITOR. I want a drink — make it a straight one.

DOCTOR. (*aggressively*) First of all, where have you come from?

VISITOR. If you don't mind, I think I've told enough stories for one night.

DOCTOR. Where are you heading for now?

VISITOR. (*thanking Marguerite, who gives him a stiff drink*) Thanks. I came here for something to eat. I was hungry.

MARGUERITE. I want to help you. If you've nothing urgent to do elsewhere, I'd like you to stay.

VISITOR. Me? Stay here? Oh no!

DOCTOR. I should hope not!

VISITOR. (*to Doctor*) I'm not going just to keep you happy.

MARGUERITE. Then why go?

VISITOR. Is there an inn near here that'd take me in if I mentioned your name? Could I get a meal with a hundred francs, and sleep in a bed with sheets and maybe have another meal tomorrow morning before I leave?

DOCTOR. Easily, with a hundred francs.

VISITOR. (*to Marguerite*) Then tell him to give me a hundred francs.

MARGUERITE. Don't leave tomorrow before you've seen me.

VISITOR. No, I want a change of air. I came here for a slice of bread. You've been too generous. You've given me a whole family, with even a young kid thrown in. That old man! I reminded him of his son. And all you could think about was him! Fussing over him as if he was a pregnant woman or something. What about me? Did you ask me if I had a father? Or a wife and kids? Well, did you, Marguerite?

MARGUERITE. What if tomorrow he asks for his son?

VISITOR. Don't bother your head about the old man. He's at peace for good. He died in my arms, still calling me his son. He's on the other side now, and maybe looking down at us this very minute. All three of us. A last backward glance before the little climb. I won't tell you my life story. That's my business. But tonight, I wish I was in the old man's shoes. Or with that fellow at the bottom of the sea. (*Marguerite is praying.*) Maybe the dead have other troubles, but at least they are new ones. (*to Marguerite, violently*) Maybe he had trouble finding out how to die. Well, me, I have trouble finding out how to live.

MARGUERITE. What can I do for you?

VISITOR. Let me go and eat. I'll feel better then. (*to Doctor*) Whose name should I give at the inn?

DOCTOR. Just go. I'll telephone.

VISITOR. Goodbye, Marguerite. My Marguerite for one night. (*exits*)

DOCTOR. He's right. It's all very well helping the dying to die, but the living also need help to live.

216

MARGUERITE. I shall wait for Paul, as his father waited for him. And when he returns . . .

DOCTOR. But he won't.

MARGUERITE. How do you know? (*train whistle*) How do you know? If the old man could still speak, he'd tell you Paul has already returned. (*softly*) Paul . . . (*on knees*) Paul!

CURTAIN